Excellent book. Maybe our next generation of corporate leaders can be encouraged by *Cookin' the Book$* to become the women and men of character America needs.
—Mark Hyatt
    Board member of the *Center for Academic Integrity (Duke University)*
    Board member of the *Character Education Partnership*

Cookin' the Book$ is light-hearted reading about a not-so-light topic. It's a charming little book that I'll be recommending to attendees at my upcoming seminars in the U.S. and Latin America entitled "Ethics after Enron."
—Professor Max Torres
    Areas of specialization include ethical decision-making models and organizational leadership
    Assistant Professor of Business Ethics and Organizational Behavior, *IESE Business School, University of Navarra, Spain* (1992-present)
    Visiting Scholar (2002-2003) and Visiting Assistant Professor (2003-2004)
    Tuck School of Business at Dartmouth

A great read. I'll never look at investing in the same way. Silver is a financial genius with a bent for telling stories. He entertains us while he shows us astonishingly simple methods to read corporate financial statements and determine for ourselves who's "cookin' the books."
—Judy Shane
    Extension Instructor
    UCLA Department of Business and Management

The style is funny and the examples are so sharp.
—*Businessworld*

Cookin' the Book$ by Don Silver is invaluable and very strongly recommended.
—*Midwest Book Review (www.midwestbookreview.com)*

Don Silver has cooked up a little gem.
—*Corporate Governance (www.corpgov.net)*

In *Cookin' the Book$* Don Silver serves up savory tales of unsavory corporate shenanigans, both past and present, to teach financial statement analysis in a palatable and even digestible form.
—Marilyn Ziemann, CPA (30 years in practice)

What an ingenious way to communicate ethical principles! This book is full of brilliant metaphors and analogies that cut to the heart of corporate accounting ethics issues. Not only is *Cookin' the Book$* a useful resource in learning the ethical scams of the day, it's a great story. It's easy to lose yourself in the dialogue and relationship between the characters and to forget that you're learning something! It's not just a reference book but a story that needs to be read from start to finish. *Cookin' the Book$* is a must read for all employees. *Cookin' the Book$* should be on the reading list for every business education classroom. Great book! I loved it!
—Mark S. Putnam
    President, *Character Training Inc.*
      (www.character-ethics.org)
    Author of *Ethics for a Modern Workforce* and
      Ethics for Success

Humorous parable.
—*Publishers Weekly*

PRAISE FOR
COOKIN' THE BOOK$

Cookin' the Book$ is quite a funny and interesting twist on what's going on in corporate accounting today. I highly recommend *Cookin'*—great book!
—Raymond M. Cochran
Director of Internal Audit, *Columbia University*
President, *Association of College and University Auditors* (1999-2000)

As an accounting professor at *Penn State* with a research interest in ethics, I am always on the lookout for outstanding books. *Cookin' the Book$* is very creative and a very good read.
—Mary Feeney Bonawitz, Ph.D., CPA
Assistant Professor of Professional Accountancy
Penn State University-Capital College
President, *American Society of Women Accountants*

Cookin' the Book$ is every bit as readable as promised. The most pleasant surprise was the number of specific, concrete suggestions for detecting corporate wrongdoing. This is the kind of real-world, yet accessible, approach to ethics that would resonate with students.
—Dr. Eugene Szwajkowski
Strategic management consultant
Adjunct Professor, Department of Managerial Studies
University of Illinois-Chicago

Cookin' the Book$ is an intellectual comedy.
—*Indiana CPA Society* (*The Link* newsletter)

Cookin' the Book$ stands alone as one of the funniest and straightforward works on business ethics in corporate America today.
—Peter McGuire Wolf, Ph.D.
www.businessethicsbalance.com

Cookin' the Book$ is entertaining, educational and easily digestible. The overall quality of the book is excellent.
—Ken Milani
Professor of Accountancy
Faculty Coordinator of Ethics Week
University of Notre Dame

A great book! I love to cook but this book gives cooking a whole new meaning!
—*AuditNet.org*

Cookin' the Book$: Say Pasta La Vista to Corporate Accounting Tricks and Fraud by Don Silver is an invaluable and very strongly recommended corporate guide to accounting fraud which takes the form of an advice guide on how to spot and avoid typical fraud secrets in corporate accounting.
—*AccountingWeb.com*

Cookin' the Book$ manages to make complicated issues crystal clear and be hilariously funny at the same time—all in a volume small enough to slip into your pocket or pocketbook. A truly winning combination!
—Marina v.N. Whitman
Professor of Business Administration and Public Policy
Gerald R. Ford School of Public Policy
University of Michigan

Cookin' the Book$ is a delicious and perfectly cooked meal delivered in tasty morsels—a full menu of dirty tricks to watch out for.
—*Business Start Page*

Don Silver's *Cookin' the Book$* is a necessary primer on the deceptive accounting practices of some contemporary firms.
—Margaret Monahan Hogan, Ph.D.
President of the *Center for Academic Integrity (Duke University)*
Founding Director of the *Center for Ethics and Public Life*
Chair of the Philosophy Department, *Kings College*

Excellent book. I couldn't put it down.
—Joseph Lee
Consumer education and economics teacher (retired)

Brilliantly written, easy to read and with words to live and invest by.
—Robert L. Rosebrock
President, *Healthy Hour Enterprises*

One of the areas of business on which I spend a great deal of time is that of ethics. This is where *Cookin' the Book$* comes in. Cleverly written and executed, every employee of a publicly held company (perhaps especially the accounting team) should read this book and be willing to question the finance and operations team about their own company's reporting procedures.
—Dave Kinnear
CEO, *dbkAssociates, Inc.*
(www.change-management-consulting.com)

Cookin' the Book$

Say Pasta La Vista to Corporate Accounting Tricks and Fraud

Don Silver

Adams-Hall Publishing
Los Angeles

Cover photo from Corbis.com

Library of Congress Cataloging-in-Publication Data

Silver, Don
    Cookin' the book$: say pasta la vista to corporate accounting tricks and fraud / Don Silver
    p. cm.
Includes index.
    ISBN 0-944708-70-6
1. Corporations—Accounting. 2. Investments. 3. Finance, Personal.
I. Title: Cookin' the books. II. Title.
HF 5686.C7 S52. 2002
657'95—dc 21
                    2002012528

First printing 2002
Printed in the United States of America
10 9 8 7 6 5

Accounting Hors D'oeuvres

"Cooking the books"—Knowingly providing incorrect information in a company's financial statements. Illegal.

"Forensic accounting"—Investigating a company's financial statements to determine where the numbers are buried in order to render evidence leading to a legal consequence.

Old Accountant Joke (Which Isn't Funny Anymore)

A CEO calls in accountants from two accounting firms trying to become the company's auditor. The CEO turns to the first accountant and asks, "How much is 1 plus 1?" The CPA answers, "2."

The CEO looks at the second accountant and again asks, "How much is 1 plus 1?" The second accountant pauses and then replies, "How much would you like it to be?"

Warren Buffet's View

"There is a crisis of confidence today about corporate earnings reports and the credibility of chief executives. And it's justified."
—Warren E. Buffett, CEO, Berkshire Hathaway Inc. (*New York Times*, July 24, 2002)

Alan Greenspan on Greed

"It is not that humans have become any more greedy than in generations past. It is that the avenues to express greed [have] grown so enormously."
—Alan Greenspan, Chairman of the Federal
   Reserve (July 16, 2002)

Arthur Levitt on the Numbers Game

"Too many corporate managers, auditors, and analysts are participants in a game of nods and winks...I fear we are witnessing an erosion in the...quality of financial reporting. Managing may be giving way to manipulation; integrity may be losing out to illusion."
—Arthur Levitt, (then) Chairman of the
   Securities and Exchange Commission
   (September 28, 1998)

The Federal Reserve on Corporate Reporting

"The softening in the growth of demand that emerged this spring has been prolonged in large measure by weakness in financial markets and heightened uncertainty related to problems in corporate reporting and governance."
—Federal Reserve Board (August 13, 2002)

Presidential Views on Accounting and Accountability

"Sometimes things aren't exactly black-and-white when it comes to accounting procedures."
—President George W. Bush (July 10, 2002)

"I believe that the officers, and especially, the directors of corporations should be held personally accountable when any corporation breaks the law...We must have complete and effective publicity of corporate affairs, so that the people may know beyond peradventure [chance] whether the corporations obey the law and whether their management entitles them to the confidence of the public."
—President Theodore Roosevelt, 1910

CONTENTS

Prologue

Prologue

Author's note: This is a work of fiction. My dad wasn't a gourmet chef like the one in this book. My dad did have an uncanny ability with the stock market. He could tell when a stock was at its high (he'd buy it) and when it had reached its low (he'd sell it). This was no fluke since I saw him do this time after time. Now let's meet the fictional chef dad in this book.

My daddy was a gourmet chef.

Once he had learned his trade, he was a master chef at some of the finest restaurants in the world and even owned his own restaurant two different times. When he was cooking, he was always thinking of his future and his family's.

It was back when he was trying in vain to create the first vegetarian T-bone steak at his restaurant that he discovered what he thought he should be doing for the rest of his life. He decided to sell his restaurant and become a private chef for the executive dining rooms of some of the largest corporations in the world. This would satisfy his need to be creative in cooking and a bit more, too.

You see my dad was always the student, wanting to learn more than how to make great food. He wanted to make money, too. He found owning a restaurant was too chancy a way to build up his nest egg.

He decided the stock market would be his avenue to success but only if he really understood the nuances of finances as he did with cooking.

Just as he studied with the masters in cooking schools and the finest restaurants, he learned from the crème de la crème of CEOs, CFOs and CPAs how the accounting books and records of the major corporations were correctly prepared and then sometimes sautéed, simmered and garnished.

He learned both the honest way and the less-than-honest ways corporate accounting is practiced.

Just before I went off to college, my dad took me aside to have a walk and talk about the financial facts of life.

The education I received that day was of greater value to me than what I later learned in four years of college and two years of business school.

That day he taught me about corporations, their money and their ways of accounting. How to spot danger signs. How to avoid them. How to maybe stop them from happening in the first place.

Here's what my daddy taught me that summer day about "cookin' the books" or as he called it, "cookin'."

The Head Chef's Son

Brief History of Cookin'

"I'm convinced that not long after fire was discovered, someone started trying to figure out how to cook the books."

—My Dad, the Head Chef

English Fishy and Chips

My dad and I were walking silently along a Southern California beach watching the waves come in. My dad bent down to get a closer look at the bubbles you see at the shoreline as the waves leave the shore and go back out.

He watched them pop, one by one. Then he started talking.

"Sea bubbles. Sooner or later, bubbles pop and deflate. Let me tell you a story about bubbles.

"A new stock comes on the market with exclusive rights in a hot area with tremendous potential. There's a public offering of the stock. Based on the accounting records, the company appears to be doing well.

"A frenzy develops and the stock jumps to tenfold its original price. But the insiders know the company isn't really making profits. The directors start selling the stock when the price is high.

"The truth about the company's unprofitable

operations becomes public knowledge. The stock price collapses and smaller investors are hurt or ruined."

Then he turned to me and said, "Name that stock."

Actually, I gave him the names of several companies. Each time he said, "That's right but it's not the one I'm thinking of."

When I ran out of guesses, he looked me in the eye and said, "Welcome to the South Sea Company Bubble of 1720.

"You can change the names, the dates and the details of the techniques, but the underlying greed of some people stays the same."

I asked him, "What was the story of this bubble of 1720? Did they even have stocks to bubble in 1720?"

This is what he told me.

"Two stockbrokers in England formed a new company known as the South Sea Company. The main asset of the South Sea Company was exclusive trading rights from England in the distant lands being 'discovered' around the world.

"Everyone wanted to get in on the ground floor of the New World Economy and the company raised lots of money selling its stock.

"The trading rights that the South Sea Company owned sounded better in the advertising than they were in reality.

"To keep the company going, fresh cash was needed to pay the bills. Its trading business wasn't going so well but the company decided there was no sense in telling people bad news about the accounting books and records. So they disguised what was going on.

"The best source of new money continued to be selling more stock. To encourage more demand for its stock, the company allowed investors to buy on the installment plan. This helped drive up the stock price even more since more buyers could buy additional stock.

"Investors were very happy as the stock price of the South Sea Company kept climbing.

"As the price of the stock went up, the company made investing even easier by allowing current investors to borrow against their existing stock to buy even more company stock. This cycle of a higher stock price, more loans and issuing more stock repeated itself again and again. And the stock price kept rising.

"Investors forgot or ignored that it's the flow of current and future profits that makes a company an attractive investment. Although the South Sea Company had trouble making profits, it was very good at having new stock certificates printed up and taking in the proceeds from new stock sales.

"The share price went from 100 in January, 1720, up to around 1,000 by July of that year.

"Then the directors of the company sold their shares and cashed out with big profits. Royalty and government officials were in the thick of it, too, as investors who knew the right time to sell.

"The last ones to find out the company had no real economic substance were the rest of the investors. By the time they realized that the emperor had no clothes in September, the stock price had crashed.

"Among those other investors was Sir Isaac Newton. Newton invested two times. On his first investment, he made a 100 percent profit. But after he sold his shares, the stock kept climbing in value. The thought of missing out on even bigger profits became too much to bear so he invested again at what turned out to be the top of the market.

"He lost a fortune the second time around and said, 'I can calculate the motions of the heavenly bodies, but not the madness of the people.'"

French Soufflé

I said, "This sounds just like what's going on today. Was stock fraud rare back in the 1700s?"

Dad smiled and told me, "There must have been something in the air in England and France that floated over the English Channel about the time of the South Sea Company Bubble.

"That might explain the French version of cookin' the books—the Mississippi Company Bubble. Some people became so rich from this venture that a new word was coined to describe their wealth—millionaire.

"That bubble almost ruined the entire French economy.

"An Englishman, John Law, controlled the Mississippi Company. He moved to Paris after escaping from prison. He had been convicted of murder for a duel.

"The company had exclusive rights to trade between France and its Louisiana Territory (this was almost a century before the Louisiana Purchase).

"John Law greatly expanded the company's rights and business ventures. All of this sounded better than it was.

"The stock price of the Mississippi Company soared from 500 in May, 1719, to 10,000 in February, 1720—just nine months later.

"Once investors realized how the company's books and records really looked, the stock went into a free-fall. By September, 1721, the price had dropped 95 percent. Sounding familiar yet?

"Although there were some economic forces that helped bring down the Mississippi Company, corporate chicanery was involved as well."

American Apple Pie

I wasn't too happy with what my dad was saying. I told him, "But that was England and France, not America."

He shook his head and started to explain. "From this fine tradition in England and France, America developed its own tradition of stock scandals and bubbles that continues with some companies to this day. We've had our own stock scandals for so long you could almost say, 'Stock scandals are as American as apple pie.' Every generation has them.

"When I was a young man, there was the Salad Oil Scandal. A company kept getting loans using its salad oil inventory as the collateral. When inspectors did come out and look into giant storage vats, they saw salad oil in them. The only problem was right below the surface of oil, water had been substituted to make it appear that there was more inventory than there really was.

"We've had software companies, life insurance companies and you name it playing with the books and in some cases making up customers to look bigger and better."

He looked very sad when he finished talking.

I remarked, "It's well and good to know about the old scandals but I want to know about the latest accounting tricks and fraud."

I'll never forget my dad's words to me the rest of that day.

He started explaining. "You don't open a restaurant just to make a profit today.

"Son, I don't remember exactly when it first started to be different. Change, if it's gradual, can kind of sneak up on you.

"Sure, greed and manipulation have always been around. But things used to be different. Investors planned on owning shares in a corporation for the long term. Management wanted employees to have a career with their company, not just a job. Officers and directors took the long view in planning out the projected course of a company.

"When did our corporations start looking more

at today than tomorrow? It was probably when large amounts of stock options for executives became more popular."

I interrupted my dad right there. I said, "You're starting to lose me. What are stock options and what's wrong with them?"

He nodded at me and continued to talk. "Stock options allow executives and others to buy company stock at a guaranteed price. An example would be the right to buy up to 1 million shares at $10 per share.

"Suppose the stock is at $5 now. That option to buy at $10 per share isn't worth anything. The stock price has to go up over $10 for the option to be profitable. That potential profit from an increase in the share price is what can put greed on the front burner. If the stock price goes up to $50 per share, that's $40,000,000 in profits here—the one million shares times the increase from $10 to $50 per share. Stock options aren't intrinsically bad. It depends on how they're used.

"When options came into vogue, executives were put to the test of temptation. The higher the value of the company stock, the greater the potential profit to an executive holding options at attractive purchase prices.

"But options don't last forever. They expire after a period of time.

"This put pressure on executives. Executives didn't want to miss out on a chance for a fortune. To cash in, they had to figure out how to make their company's stock go up in value before their options expired.

"Here are four ways to make a company (and its stock) more valuable: number one, increase revenues; number two, reduce expenses or number three, do both." He stopped talking.

I said, "I thought you said there were four ways. You only named three."

He continued. "The fourth way isn't legitimate. It's manipulating a company's books and records to make it appear that revenue is increasing or expenses are decreasing. This is what is generally meant by 'cooking the books.'

"What's going on today is simple. The main reason accounting records are being manipulated is to ensure executives benefit from stock options. Executives know three things:

1. Higher profits from increased revenue or decreased expenses make a company appear to be more profitable.

2. A more profitable company is worth more and commands a higher stock price per share.

3. A higher price for the company stock means higher personal profits for the executives holding options to buy that stock at a reduced price."

I raised my hand to get his attention and then quickly lowered it as I realized that I wasn't in school.

Or was I?

I asked my dad, "What makes an executive decide to put personal gain over the long-term welfare of the company and its investors?"

He sighed, "The two oldest five-letter words in the world—'greed' and 'money.'"

Four Basic Corporate Recipes for Cookin' the Books

"What's the big deal about executives having to certify financial statements they don't personally prepare? It has always been that way in restaurant kitchens. No matter how many chefs there are in the kitchen, there's really only one chef. The head chef. The head chef is responsible for all the cookin' that comes out of the kitchen no matter who actually prepares it."

—My Dad, the Head Chef

The ABCDs of Cookin'

I reminded my dad that I wasn't too knowledgeable about accounting jargon or concepts. I asked him if he could simplify what he meant by "cookin' the books."

He stopped walking, picked up a stick and started writing in the sand with it.

His scratchings looked like this:

1. R +
2. E –
3. R –
4. E +

He pointed to his handiwork and started explaining. "Boiled down to its essence, there are really just four recipes for cookin' the books:

    1. Increase revenues
    2. Decrease expenses
    3. Decrease revenues or
    4. Increase expenses

"Professional book cookers use these four as their starting point."

I stared at him with a puzzled look on my face.

I questioned, "Didn't you just contradict yourself? I get it that increasing revenues or decreasing expenses can improve a company's profits. But I don't understand the last two. How can *decreasing* revenues or *increasing* expenses help a company look good?"

"Good question," he answered. "It's counterintuitive to think that any company would want to make its results look worse but here's how it works and why.

"Say a company is having an all-time great year and making more profit than is necessary to satisfy any current or prospective investor. Wouldn't it be nice to be able to hold back some of that profit and shift it to another year when results weren't so hot?

"Or, think about the current environment where some companies are doing so poorly with earnings. If investors are expecting results to be lousy this year anyway, a stock price might not be harmed much by a company holding back some of this year's revenue from the accounting books or dumping extra expenses onto this year's financial statements."

This still wasn't clear to me. I drew a line in the sand with my foot next to the last two items. "Dad," I asked, "what's the payoff for companies taking this negative approach?"

"Looking even better in the future," he said. "Taking this route will increase future revenues or decrease future expenses. Either way that adds up to increased future profits.

"When some companies reduce revenue or increase expenses now, (numbers three and four here in the sand), those shifted dollars don't disappear from this year's financial statements. They get disguised for use at a later date. I call this technique 'rainy-day accounting.'"

I looked at him and asked, "Isn't that illegal?"

He erased his sandwriting with his left foot as he spoke to me. "There are two ways to cook the books," he explained. "Clearly illegal activities or using questionable, aggressive accounting techniques. Sometimes it's hard to separate the two.

"Now that you know the basics for cookin' the books, it's time you put on a cooking apron to learn how different cooks modify these four basic recipes. For your first course, let me tell you about 10 ways corporations cook revenues."

10 Ways Corporations Cook Revenues

"Which one offers the bigger incentive to book cookers? Seasoning the revenues or seasoning the expenses? Revenue wins hands down. Even though a $1 boost in revenue has the same effect on profits as a $1 reduction in expenses, seasoning revenue makes a company look bigger. No small portions here. In the money world, bigger is better."
　　　　　　　　　　　—My Dad, the Head Chef

#1
Eating Tomorrow's Meals Today

I was starting to get hungry so we went over to the pier to find a restaurant for lunch. I was in the mood for fresh fish but my dad didn't really care. I could tell he wanted to get back to my financial education and filling his belly was secondary.

While we were looking over the menu, he started talking again. "When I owned my own restaurant, at the end of each work day I counted up the day's receipts," he said. "If you asked me how much I earned today, there's no way I would've included the next day's receipts, too.

"Sometimes companies are in 'too much of a hurry' and start counting tomorrow's revenue today. As you can imagine, adding tomorrow to today can make it appear that there's a bright future...until tomorrow comes."

This made sense to me so I added, "Sort of counting your chickens before they hatch.

Right?"

Dad nodded in agreement and started to explain.

"Here's how this first book cooker works. Let's say a company signs a contract today to provide consulting or other services over a five-year period. The proper way to report this income is as it's earned in each year over the five-year period of the contract.

"Apparently, some corporations don't want to procrastinate when it comes to recognizing revenue from these long-term contracts.

"If a company 'needs' to improve this year's financial statements, they might report all of the future revenue from the contract as earnings from just this year. That's like going on a diet and saying it's okay to also eat some of tomorrow's meals today. It's not right. It's cheating.

"What makes it even worse is that companies don't even know for sure they'll collect all the revenue due to be paid to them years down the road. What if the customer goes bankrupt? So, they count all the revenue as though it were in hand today? No way that's okay."

I put down my menu. This was getting interesting. Someday I wanted to have my own consulting business creating video games. That summer I had worked for a video game company that bought another company whose financial statements greatly surprised my employer when they were finally closely reviewed after the purchase— but it was too late for them to do anything.

Hard as it was for me as a teenager to listen to my dad's advice, I realized that what he was talking about might actually be useful to me. So I asked, "Can you catch a company doing something like this?"

Dad nodded yes and said, "**Follow the money**...or the lack of it."

I shook my head to let Dad know he'd gone over my head. My idea of higher mathematics was correctly dividing up a restaurant bill with just one other person at the table. Of course I didn't expect to tax my mental abilities that day since Dad would be picking up the meal check as usual. But even thinking about number-crunching made me start to drift away so Dad had to bang a spoon against his water glass to bring me back down to earth.

He continued talking. "Here's how a company might get caught."

As he spoke, all of a sudden something clicked for me. My dad loved solving mysteries—whether it was guessing the end of a mystery book, discovering which ingredient another chef put in or solving these financial riddles.

He had an infectious enthusiasm for his subject as he spoke to me. This was going to be an interesting afternoon. He continued, "Here are the clues. If revenue goes way up because a company fastforwarded the reporting of five years' worth of revenue into just this year's, you'd expect to see more cash on hand. Or at least the company's short-term 'accounts receivable' (money due in one year or less) should go up for the current services being provided. If neither the cash nor the short-term receivables go up, be on your guard."

He smiled like the Cheshire cat. "If instead you see a company's long-term receivables going up (the money owed down the road), start **lookin' for the cookin'**. It can mean long-term sales are all being counted today, not over the longer period during which they're being earned.

"Another variation of counting the revenue too early is where a contract says to ship merchandise next year but the company delivers it this year and counts the revenue as part of this year's results."

He put down his menu and said, "Financial results affect stock prices. It's hard enough to win in the stock market when you have accurate information. Without it, you're just throwing darts at stock names with your eyes blindfolded."

"Well," I said. "When I own stocks in companies, I'll check them out but at least I won't have to worry about companies I don't own stock in."

Dad shook his head and said, "Son, that's not the case. Sometimes you'll have an investment in a solid company that's bought out by another company. What if that other company has inflated its revenue and stock value and used that bloated value to purchase the company you invested in? Your good company stock will be replaced by the bloated stock of the other company as part of the buyout. Unfortunately, you need to pay attention to more than just what you own if you're going to be in the stock market."

#2
Pretending Your Neighbor's Food is Yours

Dad was always a slow eater but now he was so busy talking he really slowed down. Whenever he had his fork in the air for more than a minute, I'd continue our family tradition of grabbing food off of a talker's plate and putting it on an eater's.

He noticed this, stopped talking and smiled.

"Son, you must be reading my mind. I was just gonna talk to you about eating off of someone else's plate.

"You want to invest in companies that have growing revenues. You want to hitch your wagon to a rising star, not a falling star.

"Company executives know this and that's why they always want the company revenues to be growing. Revenue isn't the same as profits. Revenue is the sales and other income. It's how much comes in. Profits are what's left over after the bills

34

are paid. Companies want growing profits, too, but more about that later.

"How can a company show increasing revenue if there isn't any? How about borrowing some numbers from another company?"

I thought Dad was kidding about this one but he wasn't.

He continued. "I know of one company that was hired to place advertising. They received a 20% commission for acting as the ad agent. However, when it came time to reporting revenues on the financial statements, the company decided that it would look far more impressive if the entire ad cost, not just their 20% commission, were counted as its revenue. That sure boosted revenue way up in a hurry.

"They weren't caught right away. Borrowing revenue can be tough to spot since it may not increase profits.

"Here's why. To disguise what's going on, companies that pad their revenue this way usually also increase their expenses by the same padded amount."

I interjected, "Add a dollar on the revenue side but add a dollar on the expense side. But why bother to add the expense dollar?"

Dad waved his fork in the air as he spoke. "That way they don't misstate their profits, just their revenues. As though it's okay to misstate revenue as long as you don't misstate profits. Enough of me talking. Let's see what you're digesting. Tell me in 100 words or less the incentive for a company to use another company's numbers."

He looked at me expectantly to see if I had been paying attention and really understood what he was talking about.

I took a deep breath since it has never been easy to answer his questions without anxiety. I told him, "A company whose revenue is getting bigger appears to be healthy. A growing company has a better chance to see an increase in its stock price. Executives who own stock or have stock options in this growing company can make more money."

My dad smiled and nodded his head. I was starting to get a feel for how and why accounting books are cooked and what to look for—follow the money.

Then I noticed he had stabbed my dinner roll with his fork and taken it when I was busy talking. Touché.

#3
You Scratch My Dinner Plate and I'll Scratch Yours

With dessert now on the table we each had an arm in front of our plates protecting them from a sneak attack.

As we were eating, my dad said to me, "Remember that nature show we saw last night. The animals trying to take over were always attempting to look bigger than they were to be more impressive and powerful. There are a lot of ways companies, too, can try to puff themselves up to look bigger than they are. They're trying to impress shareholders and lenders.

"This next revenue cooker takes two companies working hand in hand to make it work. A company finds another company in the same line of business. The first company says, 'You buy from me and then I'll buy the same item right back from you. No money needs to change hands. No goods or services need to change hands. But we'll both increase our gross revenue by having a sale.'"

Now it was my turn to bang a spoon against a water glass to get the floor. "Dad, what you're describing is ridiculous. Nothing of substance is going on."

He joked as he agreed with me. "Maybe that's why revenue is often called *gross* revenue."

I didn't get that one but I'm sure it was funny if you understood it. I smiled politely.

He turned serious. "These sweetheart arrangements have cropped up in different industries. The most common is in the energy field where they even have a special name for it: 'round-trip trades.' With round-trip trades, two companies buy and sell gas or power to each other at the same price but the energy never moves anywhere."

I said, "This sounds scarier than what you've already told me. Here companies feel bold enough to do these tactics with one another and try to jointly fool the public."

He looked at me and spoke softly, "Wait, we're just beginning."

#4
Borrow Lunch Money and Increase Your Revenue

Suddenly, the subject shifted to movies. My dad asked, "Have you ever seen the movie *Casablanca*?"

I nodded yes but then I blurted out, "Dad, you're actually getting me interested in knowing more about corporations and money. You're teaching me a financial self-defense course. Don't switch subjects and start talking about your favorite old movies now."

His eyes lit up as he realized I was sincere in what I was saying. Parents always want to teach their children but resistance, not openness, is what they usually encounter especially talking to an 18-year-old, like me.

"Oh," he said, "I'm not really getting off the topic...too much. Remember that scene where

Claude Rains, the police chief, gambles in the back room of Humphrey Bogart's cafe and then announces that he's closing the cafe because gambling is going on there. He says, 'It's shocking' and then the croupier hands him his winnings. Here's something you may find shocking, too.

"If you borrowed money from a bank, you wouldn't be under the delusion that you've just earned some income. You'd be aware that you're now saddled with a liability that comes along with getting the loaned funds. Right?"

I nodded in agreement.

"Well," he continued, "it's hard to imagine but a few corporate officers desperate for increased sales convince themselves from time to time that loans taken out by their corporations are actually sales. They must use the 'Little Engine that could' motivational approach. They keep saying to themselves 'I think I can, I think I can, I think I can...transform this loan into a sale.' And 'voila' as they say at the Cordon Bleu.

"Once this self-delusion takes place, then the next step is hiding the truth from shareholders and

41

others on the accounting books and records."
I thought my dad was teasing me with this one.
"Come on, no one calls loans a sale, do they?"

He raised his eyebrows and tilted his head slightly downward in response. Enough said.

#5
Buying Dinner at Your Own Restaurant Isn't a Sale

As Dad reviewed the check, he spoke to me without looking up. "This next technique can turn your stomach.

"Bottom line, if you owned a restaurant and grabbed a meal there now and then, you wouldn't be increasing the revenue of your restaurant. But that's not how it may work in the corporate world.

"Sometimes companies or their representatives form a 'buying company' to increase sales."

I had a blank look on my face as I asked for an explanation. "Dad, you lost me again. What's a buying company?"

He tapped his spoon on the table in a rhythm of his own as he deadpanned his explanation.

43

"A buying company," he said, "is a company that really doesn't buy anything."

I laughed and said, "Oh, *now* I understand!"

He laughed with me as he continued. "The sad part is I'm not kidding. A buying company doesn't actually pay money for the goods or services it buys from the original company. Instead, it just owes money that will never be collected. The amount owed on the purchases will be written off as a bad account down the road with the hope that no one remembers what went on."

I still wasn't clear on this so I asked, "Who forms a buying company?"

He replied, "A buying company might be formed by the officers or directors of a company or persons involved with them."

"Why have a buying company?" I asked. "It seems like much ado about nothing," I said proudly showing off some of my high school education.

"Come on, son, you live in Southern California. You know how important appearances are. These phony sales look the same as real sales and provide a financial facelift. They appear to be generating real revenue and give a new look to the financial statements.

"It's just that there's not a Hollywood ending here. The reality is that a company is just selling something to itself and that usually comes out in the end. The financial statements get an artificial appearance from all of this and in time start to sag. That's when everyone knows for sure that something was doctored."

He stood up, left a generous tip on the table and gestured for me to exit with him. I wanted to tell him that he had already given me plenty of food for thought but I didn't want to get him started on his puns.

#6
Giving a Free Lunch Doesn't Increase Sales

As we were walking out of the restaurant my dad saw a sign that said, "There's no such thing as a free lunch."

He pointed to the sign and said, "That's the truth. I spoke a moment ago about companies selling to their own buying companies. Now I'll tell you about 'homing pigeon sales' to their usual customers—real companies.

"Here's where the free lunch comes in. Sometimes companies change their sales policy and deliberately make sales where the purchasing company can't afford to pay for them or where there's a side letter saying they really don't have to pay for them.

"The company receiving the goods feels like it's Christmas or the day after Christmas. They can return anything they want for a full credit with a homing pigeon sale—it goes back to the selling

46

company. This takes all the risk out of purchasing."

I pointed out, "Isn't that a good way to increase business?"

"Maybe," he responded. "Suppose you went into a restaurant and were told you could order as much as you wanted but you'd only have to pay for the items you finished. You might go hog wild and order everything on the menu. At the end of your meal the restaurant wouldn't be able resell what you didn't finish. It'd be wasted food and wasted profit.

"It can be the same with these homing pigeon sales. With this type of sale, the seller *expects* the goods to end up coming back home and the sales are pre-programmed to do so. If customers have no penalty for overbuying and can return everything, they'll take everything they can. The penalty is on the 'selling' company. It has to pay for the production of extra goods to meet the extra 'demand,' the shipping costs and the bad inventory. By the time they're returned, the goods might be damaged, too old or out of style.

"About the only business that functions like this

as a normal matter of course (and it doesn't function that well) is the book business where bookstores can return virtually anything to publishers. Bookstores may be in the book business but that isn't the same as 'cookin' the books.' It's just the usual way that industry functions."

Once again I was missing something here. "Homing pigeon sales don't make sense to me," I said. "Why would companies knowingly make sales that will just be returned?"

Dad said, "If sales count this year and returns are counted next year, this recipe provides a short-term energy boost to the financial statements.

"Here's where I get suspicious," Dad continued. "If a company adopts a new policy and starts extending very liberal credit or full return privileges to its customers, it can be a sign that the sales aren't real or the demand for the company's product is so weak that extraordinary measures need to be taken to boost sales."

As we walked out the front door of the restaurant, I kept this thought to myself—I had just gotten a free lunch, thanks to Dad.

#7
Separating the Wheat from the Chaff

The sea air felt great as we went back to walking along the beach. We saw a father pitching a tennis ball to his young son who was trying to hit it with a tiny bat. My dad nodded in their direction and smiled as it brought back fond memories for both of us.

"The first thing I taught you about baseball," he said, "was to keep your eye on the ball. It's the same with investing and looking at a company's financial statements. The strike zone you want a company concentrating on is the 'core' of a company's business. That's where you're most interested in seeing how the numbers add up. Are they hitting home runs? Singles? Or striking out most of the time?

"With a software manufacturer, you want to know how the software sales and expenses are doing. That's the core of the business to focus on.

"Sometimes companies will try to expand their strike zone by counting pitches outside of it."

I thought Dad was getting a little carried away with his baseball analogy so I questioned him. "Dad, what are you trying to say?"

He didn't answer me at first. Instead he reached down, picked up a big rock and tossed it high in the air. When it came down he snatched it with a quick forward motion of his hand rather than using an easier palms up catch. Then he also picked up a small rock, threw both rocks in the air and was able to snatch both of them in quick succession as they came down. That was pretty impressive. I figured he developed this skill when he was learning to throw pizza dough in the air and catching it before it hit the floor.

Finally, he answered my question. "If this big rock is the income from a company's core operations, its 'operating income,' that's the one you want to keep your eye on. If the small rock is 'investment income' from how a company invests its unused cash, that income usually isn't as central to a company's future.

"With some companies you need to follow the

bouncing ball. Companies sometimes pitch investment income over to the sales revenue column where it doesn't belong. Investment income like interest and dividends doesn't belong with the sales revenue of a company. Separate the wheat from the chaff and always, always, keep your eye on the ball."

He threw both rocks back in the air, caught the big one and then turned his back and walked away as the small rock thumped on the ground behind him.

#8
Getting In On the Gravy Train

We walked along and made some small talk. I saw two teenagers tossing a football around. One of them missed a catch and the ball came rolling towards us.

My dad had played quarterback in high school and his love for the game had never diminished. I'm sure he still imagined himself playing on the field when he watched games on TV.

He picked up the ball and yelled out to the kid farthest away. "Go deep, run a post pattern." The kid took off and started running hard. Dad reared back and shot a bullet through the air. The spiral came down perfectly to the outstretched hands of his receiver and Dad raised both of his arms to symbolize a touchdown. He had a big smile on his face.

"There's nothing like making a big play," he said. "Imagine there's only time for one play and your team is deep in your own territory. The only way to win is to throw a bomb. A big pass for a big play. There's no time for little gains here and there. It's all or nothing time.

"Unfortunately, rather than report bad financial results when their backs are up against the wall, some company officials go for the bomb. They try to score in one play by creating one big gain that will save the day and win the game."

I asked, "What kind of gain are you talking about?"

Dad responded. "The big gain comes from the sale of an asset like real estate. This isn't income from the company's core operations. If company officials are desperate to raise profits and the stock price to get on the stock option gravy train, this gain goes offside and ends up in the wrong place. Instead of being reported as a one-time gain unrelated to the company's operations, it's buried and reported as part of the core operating income."

He bent down and picked up a flat rock and started tossing and catching, tossing and catching.

"Ah," he said, "football is so pure. All the action takes place in public view right in front of the fans and with the officials right on top of the action. If the rules aren't followed, a penalty is called and the punishment is dished out immediately."

I suddenly realized why he loved sports like baseball, football and basketball so much. Sure he admired great individual efforts and that how they were blended together as a team determined the results. But there was also a quest for fairness in sports with umpires and referees who are an integral part of the games. That's what was missing for him in some cases in the financial world and it was painful for him to see this.

#9
Scrambled
Nest Eggs

Dad was kind of pumped up from his touchdown throw. We walked briskly past a group of senior citizens who had set up a card table with chairs to play cards on the beach.

They were having a good time, laughing and joking, enjoying the beach and also probably not having to go to work anymore. I was in a completely different place. I was looking forward to getting my first real job. Retirement seemed so far away for me.

Seeing that group of retiree card players made Dad think of his next question for me. "What," he asked, "do you know about pension funds?"

"Not much," I admitted. "What are they?"

Dad responded. "You know your grandfather worked for the same company for 40 years and he receives a payment each month from the company since he retired."

I nodded in agreement. Grandpa was always telling me to save for my retirement. I would tell him, "I'm only 18 years old. What's the rush?" Grandpa would always counter, "You can't start too early."

"Well," Dad continued, "Grandpa was part of a pension fund at work. His employer guaranteed him in retirement a certain percentage of his income based on his salary and how long he worked there."

"He sure worked there a long time," I added.

Dad nodded in agreement. "Grandpa's pension plan was paid for completely by the company. This type of pension plan, a 'defined benefit pension plan,' is still very common. It's different than the newer, increasingly common 401(k) plan where the employee pays in the bulk of the retirement money.

"What I'm going to talk about next is Grandpa's type of pension plan. It's still around especially at larger companies. The money his company contributed to the plan and the growth on the investments made with the money are known as the pension funds."

My dad kept walking and was lost in his own thoughts as he looked out to where the sky and the ocean met in the distance. Then he turned to me and asked, "Would you guess that pension funds are a small, medium or huge amount of money?"

I answered, "Obviously a huge amount" and right then I knew my financial horizon was going to be expanded. So I asked him, "Dad, what can companies do to manipulate pension funds?"

"Gains or losses in pension fund accounts affect a company's profits," he said. "They're not completely separate. They affect corporate finances.

"A really big gain in pension investment results can not only eliminate a company's need to make a contribution that year and thereby reduce expenses, it can also generate income on top of that. The category that income is put in on a financial statement either reports or distorts the results.

"Pension income can be so important in some cases that a company may buy another company mainly to get credit on their own books for the sterling performance of the other company's pension fund."

I looked back at the group playing cards and thought of Grandpa, too. I wondered if life had been so complicated for him when he was growing up. I also made a note in my mind to call Grandpa to see how he was doing.

#10
Everything But
the Kitchen Sink

We turned around to head back towards the pier. It was getting pretty hot out there on our walk.

"Dad," I asked, "is there any limit as to what can be buried or disguised as revenue?"

He walked towards an incoming wave to cool off his feet and started talking. "If company officials are determined, they can try to call almost anything revenue. Loans. Consignment sales. Refunds for defective goods. Leases. Disputes. Even lawsuit settlements against them."

"Lawsuit settlements as revenue?" I exclaimed.

"Yes," he replied. "I heard of one instance where a company shipped another company merchandise to pay off a lawsuit settlement and called it sales revenue."

"How," I wondered, "can anyone even come up with an idea like that?"

Dad answered me. "Most people are under the impression that only dull, unimaginative individuals are involved with accounting and financial statements. Nonsense. Maybe that's why we're always surprised like it's the first time when we hear of a financial guise. Novelists or science fiction writers could learn a lot from studying the plot lines of some financial statements.

"Son, we've covered 10 revenue cookin' techniques. There are actually lots more but they're all basically a variation on these ten."

With that he put cooking lessons on the back burner and kicked some water up to splash me in the face. That started a drag-down, all-out water fight between us. It sure felt good with that hot sun pouring down on us.

Dad knew when it was time to get out of a hot kitchen and take a break. I sure was ready.

10 Ways Corporations Cook Expenses

"The only real difference between cookin' revenues and cookin' expenses is that you use different financial utensils. They both leave a bad taste in your mouth."

—My Dad, the Head Chef

#1
Remaking Yesterday's Dinner Today

We were completely drenched from our water fight but feeling refreshed. We sat out on the sand to dry out.

Dad wanted to take a nap. That sounded good to me. While we were both laying back with our eyes closed, Dad asked me, "Have you ever had a bad experience and tried to change the outcome in a dream?"

This had happened to me every night for a week after I took the SAT so I knew what he was talking about. Dad opened his eyes to look at me.

"Son, this can happen to corporations, too. They try to make their dreams come true. It starts out where financial results aren't so good this year. In their desperation the only way company officials can think of to make things better this year is to push current expenses to an earlier year and dump the damage there. The company does this by 'restating its earnings.'"

"What do you mean," I asked, "by restating its earnings?"

"That's where," he said, "a company makes a retroactive change to its financial statements. It could be a change in the revenue, the expenses, the assets, the liabilities or some or all of these. In this case, it'd be saying these current expenses should've been counted in an earlier year."

"Whoa," I interjected. "What does that do to investors who thought the company was doing better in the prior years and bought some shares?"

"Sometimes," he answered, "it makes them feel like they've been having a bad dream."

#2
What's the Daily Special?

Once again we saw the father and son playing baseball. They had switched from batting practice to playing catch. The young boy had trouble catching most of the throws but he kept getting words of encouragement from his dad as he tried again and again.

My dad pointed to them and said, "Part of the enduring appeal of baseball is that every year, the teams and players get a fresh chance with a new season. Their win/loss record or their batting average always starts over each new season. This means, at least at the beginning of a season, there can always be hope that this new year will be a good year.

"Mergers of companies are like that, too. Companies want to start a new financial season after a merger. Clear the decks. Clean up the financial messes. One way to do this is to take a one-time special charge."

Here was that accounting jargon again. It might be second nature to my dad but it sure wasn't to me. To me a "one-time special charge" was using his credit card for a major purchase he'd disapprove of later. I didn't think that was what he was talking about so I asked, "Dad, please explain one-time special charges."

Dad walked towards the breaking waves. He built up a tall pile of sand and the next wave washed it away leaving no trace of its existence.

"That," he said as he pointed to the empty spot, "is a one-time special charge. It's there one moment and suddenly, it's gone forever. Here's how it works with mergers. Right after a merger, a company lumps in expenses it expects to incur in the future related to the merger and says in effect:

> Things were bad under the prior management. To clean things up we'll incur some expenses. We'll deduct them now as a one-time special charge.

"For legitimate merger-related expenses, that's okay. The problem comes when a one-time special charge is built up to include more expenses than it should."

I was puzzled again. "Doesn't that make the company look bad, adding extra expenses?" I asked.

Dad shook his head. "No. Everyone assumes that the special charge for these extra expenses is due to prior mismanagement. Knowing this, new management sometimes tries to write off as much expense as possible to wipe the slate clean and then some.

"Sometimes things get way out of hand where new management basically says to itself:

> Wouldn't it be nice to deduct future years' expenses now and blame them on pre-merger conditions and management? That way we'll reduce expenses in future years by deducting them now and look even more profitable down the line.

"Because it's a one-time charge, it's often seen as an aberration, something unusual that doesn't reflect negatively on the future of the company.

"Sometimes those inflated expenses include writing off or writing down the value of an asset."

He looked at me to see if I recognized what he was talking about. I'm sure my face screamed out, "Not a clue. Not a clue." Seeing my blank expression prompted him to explain.

"When an asset is written off or written down, the company is saying the asset isn't worth anything or at least not as much as previously shown on the financial statements. It's a way of taking a big expense all at one time by expensing the asset way down or down to zero. The problem is where more is expensed than should be."

I saw an opening and took it. "Sort of like pretending a prepaid phone card is all used up when it isn't."

"Right," he said, "and when the phone card works in the future, you call it a gain or some other form of revenue. This is a way to distinguish the new management as being so much more successful than the old regime."

I got this now. "Dad, is this like finding a financial scapegoat and pinning all the blame there you can?"

As I said this he was watching the father and son.
The boy made a great catch and his dad broke
into a smile from ear to ear. My dad looked at me
and smiled, too, and gave me a big pat on the
back. He was telling me how proud he was of my
catching on to all of this financial talk.

His praise made me feel good. I guess it doesn't
matter how old you are. If you look good in your
dad's eye, that still means something. That's when
I first considered majoring in accounting. I
thought I was beginning to show a natural talent
for understanding this sort of stuff. Maybe I
could become a financial detective and right the
financial wrongs of the world.

#3
Mislabeling
the Ingredients

Dad started walking faster and faster and I asked why. "To work off lunch," he responded.

While I huffed and puffed, he charged ahead without breaking a sweat or showing any sign that this was any exertion for him. So much for youth. Maybe I better cut back on those pastries and start working out instead, I thought.

Dad said something to me but I couldn't hear him because I was too far behind. He stopped to let me catch up and he repeated himself.

"Special one-time charges aren't restricted to mergers," he said emphatically.

I never said they were, I thought to myself.

He started walking fast again and I forced myself to keep up with him.

"Although," he started again, "special charges can

be used correctly to report unusual expenses, they can also be misused to disguise regular, expected expenses. When this happens, future expenses are incorrectly deducted in the current period."

I raised my right hand to get his attention to slow down his walking. He thought I was indicating I didn't understand what he was saying. As long as he stopped, I didn't care why.

"Well, it's like this," he explained. "If investors see expenses labeled as a special charge, a special expense, they think it's a rare occurrence that won't happen again. They may not hold it against management in reviewing its performance or in evaluating the value of a company. By contrast, if a company has everyday problems rather than these rare special problems, that's when things may start to boil over. That's where the temptation comes for companies to mislabel everyday expenses as special expenses or charges.

"Hey," he said, "let's slow down for a while and cool off." I couldn't have agreed with him more as I wheezed to a complete halt.

#4
Preserves
and Reserves

I was going to be flying out alone the next day to get settled in my new school. Going off to college by myself made me feel quite grown up. Then I realized I hadn't made the plane reservation myself. My dad had. Oh, well. Who says I have to be an adult now anyway?

Dad broke my train of thought with a question. "What do you know about reserves?"

I was probably still lost in my own thoughts because I thought he had asked me what I knew about "preserves."

I answered, "Don't you add sugar to fruit and cook them?"

Dad looked at me like I was from Mars. I exclaimed, "Isn't that how you make preserves?" I thought a chef's son should know this.

Dad had a good laugh with that one. He said, "I

asked you about reserves, not preserves. When you start looking at financial statements, you'll see the word 'reserve' or its equivalent all over the place."

Now there was a pleasant thought. Looking at financial statements.

"There is a reserve for bad debts called the 'allowance for doubtful accounts,'" he continued. "Reserves for inventory. Reserves for depreciation. There are enough reserves to field an entire team."

I got the sports analogy but I really didn't have any idea what he was talking about. Again it showed on my face. I thought I better work on this or all the college professors would be able to spot me whenever I didn't know the answer to a question.

"Don't you know what all these reserves are?" he asked me.

I shook my head.

"It's not a perfect world," Dad said. "Customers don't always pay the amount they owe so a 'bad debt reserve' estimates how much of the 'accounts receivable' (the money that's owed by customers) will go bad.

"Inventory doesn't always get sold, stay fresh or stay in fashion. A reserve for inventory estimates how much of the inventory will ultimately be unsalable. On and on it goes.

"Companies are making estimates with reserves for the amounts that they expect to write off as an expense. If the reserves turn out to be larger than the estimated costs, the unused reserve is reclassified to increase earnings."

Thinking of my prepaid telephone cards I said, "You probably have set up a reserve in your mind as to how much of the phone cards' value I'll waste either by not using them up before they expire or by losing them."

He couldn't hide his thoughts either on this one. I'd been known to misplace cell phones, credit cards and even an automobile once. Do you know how long it takes for all of the cars at a baseball stadium to leave before you can locate a car by process of elimination? Do you know how nervous you can get when it's your father's car that's missing?

He interrupted my thoughts when he spoke. "Here's what can happen with reserves. A company is setting up its accounting books and records for the year. They want to accurately reflect the status of the business. They're thinking of using a $50 million reserve for bad debts. That means for all of the money owed to them, their accounts receivable, they expect $50 million to be uncollectible. That's a $50 million expense.

"If that reserve were revised to $20 million, that's saying $30 million of previously thought uncollectible receivables will be collectible. That reduces expenses, the bad debt expenses, for the current year by $30 million and the reduced expenses mean $30 million in additional profits."

"Does that mean," I asked, "you need to be on the lookout for reserves that are too small?"

"Yes and no," he answered. "The game can also be played the other way, too. If a company is having too good a year, it may set up an oversized reserve for bad debts. That reduces the current year's income.

"Then, in the years to come, the company can get an extra boost of income from reducing the size of the reserves. That reduces that year's expenses. When the financial statements are manipulated this way, it's like turning a money faucet on and off as needed. This is an example of the rainy-day accounting I spoke about earlier when I gave you the four basic recipes for cookin' the books. The problem with trying to see accurate numbers shown in reserves is that reserves are estimates and the guidelines for calculating reserves are not always clear."

I suddenly had a thought. "Dad, what do you think of this? Reserves may be as important as the first team."

Dad beamed at me and said, "I think he's got it."

#5
Mixing Ingredients in the Right Order

I had some money questions for Dad that didn't deal with corporate financial statements. He had told me that while I was in college I'd be responsible for managing my own bank account and paying for tuition, books, dorm charges and living expenses from it. I asked him about his system for organizing bills and paying them on time. Then he asked me a question.

"Will you be paying your tuition as the bills come in or years in advance?" he questioned.

I wasn't sure if this was a trick question but I answered it straight. "As they come in." I was waiting for the other shoe to drop but it didn't.

Dad started talking again. "Bills for a company need to be paid on time but do they need to be paid a year or two in advance? If a company prepays expenses too far in advance, it may be trying to reduce income in the current period to make future periods look better.

"That's why I always keep an eye on prepaid expenses on financial statements. Ordinarily, companies like to delay paying expenses as long as possible. If, instead, prepaid expenses are going up, there better be a good reason why. Hopefully, it's not that the company has written off perform-ance in the current period so much that they decide to trash it and create a big turnaround in the upcoming years."

Dad explained. "Let me give you an example closer to home. You know those phone cards you're taking with you to college that have a preset amount of long-distance dollar value on them?"

I nodded.

"Well," he continued, "wouldn't you wonder about your dad if I bought you enough prepaid cards to last you ten years?"

Actually that sounded pretty good to me. Maybe, I thought, I shouldn't be majoring in accounting at college this fall.

#6
Finding the Missing Ingredient

Dad started digging furiously in the sand. Once he had scooped out a hole, he placed a rock in it. Then he pushed the pile of sand back on top of rock until it was completely covered.

He pointed to his handiwork and said, "Here's a popular cookin' technique. Improve the bottom line by burying expenses in a non-expense category."

The way Dad was using whatever was available to him on the beach to make his points made me think that he must do the same in the kitchen— taking the available ingredients and mixin' and matchin' them to produce whatever he had in his mind. The only limit was his imagination. I was having a new appreciation for his creativity. I had always thought that brain cells started to die rapidly when someone got old, like in their 40s, and creativity sort of shriveled up then.

Dad started to explain. "Suppose a company

owns its office buildings and has maintenance and normal repairs on them. That's a normal operating expense that reduces profits dollar for dollar.

"However, sometimes these expenses are transformed on financial statements from an expense into an asset. Isn't that a neat trick? In this case real estate expenses would be transformed on the books into a real estate asset. Then the company would deduct these operating expenses piecemeal over time rather than all at once."

He stuck his hand down into sand and pulled up the rock. "Sometimes," he said, "it takes some digging to find this out on the financial statements."

#7
Crockery Pot Accounting—Doing the Slow Simmer

Dad sat up and started drawing in the sand again. This time it looked like a cooking pot with a top on it and dollar signs floating out of the edges as steam. He was no great shakes as an artist but I could decipher what he was drawing.

He started talking as he put the final touches on his Mona Lisa. "A favorite way to cook expenses is what I call 'crockery pot accounting.' Even if the accounting rules say you should bring expenses to a boil, with this recipe you just let expenses simmer, cook slowly and tip the lid just enough so they evaporate over time."

Although I was feeling pretty good about understanding his points so far, I made a request. "Can we keep it simple and not talk about big corporations here?"

Dad said, "Sure. Let's talk about a neighborhood restaurant. The principles are the same; it's the magnitude of the dollars that's different.

"Say I own a restaurant along with some partners and expect to take in $250,000 in revenue this year and pay out $200,000 in expenses for rent, salaries, food and utilities. So far, it looks like there will be $50,000 in profits. Right?"

I nodded yes.

"Then," Dad said, "I get the idea to try to boost sales by instituting an aggressive new advertising program for this year that will cost $50,000. I wouldn't jump at that right away. If all of that advertising cost is taken as an expense this year and sales don't increase, my $50,000 profit would evaporate to zero. I wouldn't be happy with that and neither would my partners who had invested in my restaurant.

"Suppose I convinced myself that, 'Investors won't see it that way. Even though I'm spending $50,000 this year, what if I don't count it all as an expense this year? Instead, when figuring profit or loss, what if I spread out the $50,000 in advertising costs evenly over a 10-year period and just count $5,000 per year as a cost for the next 10 years?'

"That's known as 'capitalizing' an expense. With just $5,000 deducted as a current expense, my partners would think my restaurant had a $45,000 profit for the current year."

This triggered lots of thoughts in my mind and I spit out several questions in rapid fire. "Wouldn't you be fooling your partners if you did that? What's the right thing to do here? Deduct it all this year or spread it out over time? How do you know what to do?"

Dad looked me in the eye and answered. "An accountant would give the answer by looking at GAAP," he said as he spelled out the letters one by one.

SAT. NCAA. Now GAAP. I said, "What's GAAP? A kind of accountant alphabet soup that floats around and spells out the right answer in your bowl?"

He laughed as he started to explain. "GAAP stands for 'generally accepted accounting principles.' These are the rules the accounting profession has established so accountants and corporate officials know the do's and don'ts when it comes to accounting for the company's books. Although the rules provide some flexibility, they provide guidelines, too.

"If the expenses here are slow cooked over 10 years and not brought to a boil and deducted all this year, the accountants call this 'capitalizing expenses.' When an expense is capitalized, it isn't deducted all at once. The deduction is spread out over time."

I interjected, "You still haven't answered me. What would GAAP have to say about this scenario?"

Dad continued. "It says that companies should deduct it all right away unless there's a real good reason to believe costs like this can be linked to revenues occurring over a multi-year time period. In a case like we're talking about here, I would be trying for an immediate, short-term boost in revenues, not a 10-year plan. That would tell me to deduct it all at once and expense it all this year.

"But not every restaurant owner would come to the same conclusion. That's when the aroma or stink of cookin' expenses fills the air."

I spoke up here to see if I understood all this. "So

some businesses heat up the revenue but just simmer the expenses?"

Dad got up to stretch and start walking before he responded in his typical corny style, "Son, you've hit it right on the money."

#8
Going Beyond the Expiration Date

We resumed walking along the shoreline. A jogger came towards us whose face looked at least 75 years old but whose body looked only 35.

Dad and the jogger nodded to one another.

Dad commented, "Although not everyone wants to live forever, there are lots of people who want to extend their lives a few more years. Some companies are like that, too, with their expenses if they use 'Ponce de Leon accounting.' It's the quest for the fountain of youth so expenses live beyond their normal expiration date."

I popped up here. "Isn't this what you just spoke about with the advertising cost?"

"This is different," he answered. "With the advertising cost, it was clear that all of the expense should've been deducted in one year. With the 'life extension technique' I'm talking about here, an expense should be deducted over more than one year but the question is how many more years."

"What's an example?" I inquired.

"Research and development costs," he said, "that are incurred by a company when it is first trying to produce a software product. Should the costs be deducted over two years? Five years? Or some other length of time?"

"And the payoff for a longer life?" I asked.

He responded, "That's the right question. The longer the 'useful life,' the less that's used up each year and needs to be deducted, expensed, each year."

He had said a mouthful but I hadn't gotten a full earful. So I spoke up again before he went any further. I simply said, "I don't get it."

Dad had a lot of patience. That's probably why he was known not only as a great chef but as a great teaching chef. He laid it out for me step by step. "If a company picks five years instead of three years for allocating these research and development expenses, it's deducting less in expenses each year—it's deducting one-fifth each year for five years instead of one-third each year over three years.

"Let's say there are $15 million in expenses. To divide that up evenly over three years is $5 million in expenses per year. Over five years that comes to $3 million in expenses per year. The longer life, the five-year useful life, reduces expenses by $2 million each year the first three years and boosts profits by the same amount."

I tried to put all of this together and restate it back to him. "Gain today and be gone tomorrow?"

Boy did he like that one. Yikes! Now I was starting to talk like him.

#9
Quenching Your Thirst

My dad was thirsty from all of this talking so we walked across the sand to the boardwalk to find him a drinking fountain. He turned the handle on the fountain and a tremendous amount of water shot out. Then he adjusted the handle too far the other way and it became just a trickle. Finally, he found the right amount of pressure to quench his thirst.

As he wiped his mouth dry with his left hand, he pointed with his right hand to the drinking fountain and said, "That's how pension plans work on financial statements."

I had a puzzled frown on my face.

"Remember Grandpa's pension plan we spoke about earlier?" Dad asked.

I gave a quick nod as it came back to me. With Grandpa's plan, the company paid for everything, making all of the contributions.

Dad continued. "Traditionally, each year companies estimate in advance how much growth and earnings there will be in their pension plan assets. They may assume a 9% or 10% increase and base their contribution on that rate of return.

"The higher the estimated rate of return, the lower the company's contribution needs to be. A lower contribution means less pension expense and higher profits." I looked puzzled again.

"Let's say a company wants to end up with $110 million in pension plan assets by the end of the year and they already have $100 million at the beginning of the year. If they estimate a 10% return, no contribution will be needed from the company that year. The $100 million in assets will grow by 10%, $10 million. If the company estimates a 5% return, $5 million, from earnings, the company will have to contribute the difference, $5 million, to meet its goal."

"Aren't all estimates wrong," I asked, "since no one can predict something like that with certainty?"

I was rewarded with another one of his beaming smiles.

"Of course," he answered. "Here's where the cookin' comes in. If the company is too optimistic and the actual results are worse than the estimates, the company has to pony up the extra funds to make up that shortfall. But that horseplay will take place in the following year and the extra expense will land there, not in the current year.

"And with the stock market down so much, some companies may struggle to replenish their pension plan because of the drop in value of pension investments. The footnotes to the financial statements should disclose any shortfalls.

"Remember if a company's goal is to boost profits this year, then accuracy or the ultimate cost of paying expenses next year isn't as important."

We needed to recross the boardwalk to get back to the shoreline. While we were dodging skaters and bike riders, I thought about estimates. We were making estimates as to who would hit us if we crossed in their path and calculating how fast we needed to move to get across safely. I hadn't realized until today how important estimates were in accounting. I had always assumed everything there was black and white. I was learning a lot.

#10
Keeping Track of the Essential Ingredients

My sweet tooth called out to me when I saw an ice cream vendor next to the boardwalk. Dad had more willpower than me but I took a double scoop of chocolate chip.

I was lucky. It was such a hot day the vendor told us, "That's it. You're my last customer. I'm sold out."

Dad spoke to me. "Do you know what you're eating? To you, it's ice cream." Then he pointed to the vendor closing up his cart and taking down his umbrella. "To him, it's inventory.

"Inventory is a very special asset on financial statements. It plays a central role in determining a company's profit or loss.

"Take my word for it—the upward or downward direction of a company's ending inventory makes profit travel in the same direction. Ending inventory is part of a calculation for how much of the total inventory cost should be allocated to sales. It's part of the equation for what's called the 'cost of goods sold.'"

This was all fine and good but "what does 'ending inventory' mean?" I asked my Dad.

"You file your income taxes based on a calendar year. Companies can also have a calendar year or they can use a different time period, a 'fiscal year,' to keep track of their results. For example, a company might have a year that runs from July 1 through June 30. The ending inventory for that company's year would be its inventory on June 30.

"If the ending inventory goes up, so does its profit. Likewise, if the ending inventory goes down, the company's profit goes down. Maybe that's why sometimes desperate companies fake inventory like putting bricks in boxes."

"Bricks?" I asked.

"Yes," he responded. "Remember when I told you about the Salad Oil Scandal of the 1960s where inventory was faked to get loans by substituting water for oil in giant oil vats?"

I nodded yes.

He continued. "One disk drive manufacturer tried to increase its ending inventory to boost profits. When the auditors came around to check up on things, they lifted up boxes of inventory to make sure there was real inventory. Well, the weight was real but the boxes contained bricks, not disk drives. The auditors had only lifted the boxes, not opened them. Who would've thought a company would try to fool its auditors like this? That substitution wasn't discovered until later."

Apparently college wasn't the only place I'd be getting an education. The world out there was to be a great teacher.

A Financial Self-Defense "Menual"

20 Tips for Getting Around the Corporate Kitchen

"Lincoln said, 'You can fool some of the people all of the time, and all of the people some of the time but you can not fool all of the people all of the time.' Son, I don't want *anyone* foolin' you *any* time."

—My Dad, the Head Chef

#1
If Management Won't Eat the Food, Should You?

The sun was starting to sink lower in the sky. This was the last night I'd be living at home. This was a big step for me, going off to college. I knew my dad would miss me a lot and I'd miss him, too.

If only my mom had lived long enough to see this day, she would've been so happy. It's hard to have a lot of history when your mom dies and you're only two years old. But I felt I knew her and her love for me through stories my dad told me about her and stories he related about her and me.

Dad had a pretty tough job raising me alone. While I never did see Dad's feminine side, I always felt his love for me. And he was never shy in expressing it in words, too.

On the surface Dad was giving me important information that afternoon I'd use the rest of my life. Years later I realized this talk was more important to him on a symbolic level. He was trying to teach me how to protect myself when he wouldn't be around, when he'd join my mom.

That's probably why he had a sad look on his face until he caught me staring at him. He quickly put on a big smile as he continued his financial self-defense manual or, as he called it, his "*menu*al." You can take the chef out of the kitchen but you can't take the kitchen out of the chef.

"Suppose," he said, "you're at a restaurant. At the next table is the owner of the restaurant. He's in your line of sight. The waiter is by your table and he's ready to take your order.

"You say, 'I'll have the fresh fish of the day.' The restaurant owner looks at you, silently shakes his head and then holds his nose.

"You change your order to 'the Chicken Alfredo.' The restaurant owner shakes his head and rolls his eyes."

Dad could always get a laugh out of me and he did this time, too.

Dad laughed, too, as he continued. "Just like it'd

be nice to have this kind of inside information before you placed a dinner order, it'd be nice to know whether corporate insiders are selling their stock before you place your stock order."

"Dad," I asked, "what are corporate insiders?"

He answered. "Corporate insiders include officers, directors, lawyers, accountants, stock-brokers and others who know non-public information about a company's situation. The law penalizes insiders who take advantage of significant inside information and use it for their personal benefit. It's not like they can never sell their company stock but there are special rules for them. Wouldn't it get your attention if all the corporate officers were selling the company stock while at the same time telling the public how great the stock is?"

"Sure would," I responded. "But how can anyone find out what insiders are doing? Do they take out ads and say 'look at what I'm selling today'?"

"Sort of," Dad said. He surprised me with that answer. "A lot of that insider information is available on the Net," he told me. "Look at the Securities and Exchange Commission's website at www.sec.gov. And you can also go to the major financial sites, find a company's stock listing and click on the 'Insiders' tab.

"Bottom line, before you jump in and buy a stock, take a look at what the insiders are doing. Are they sticking around or holding their noses and running as far away as possible?

"After all, if management doesn't want to eat there anymore, do you?"

#2
Avoid Leftovers

We climbed up the stairs towards the arcade on the pier. I was a little surprised we were going there. Dad never cared much for arcades. He felt that some of the barkers gave you a pitch that enticed you to put down your money and then they took it without giving you an even chance. Although he was sure most of them were honest, he always said it was difficult for him to separate the legits from the crooks.

Dad broke up my thoughts with a new topic. "We've been talking just about the company accounting side of things. I want to pass on a few observations from the investor's point of view. These aren't investing tips. They're more the psychology of investing."

"Dad," I responded, "what does this have to do with spotting accounting tricks and fraud?"

"You need," he said, "to reduce your susceptibility to tricks and fraud by becoming a more conscious, a more aware investor. That's the connection."

101

We saw a crowd gathered around a wheel of fortune.

Dad pointed to the group of people and said, "Don't order yesterday's main course. If everybody else is excited and talking about how good a stock is, it's probably too late for you to invest in it. Let me tell you a story.

"Remember those stock bubbles we talked about at the start of our walk?" Dad said. "Sometimes people want to see value or substance where there isn't much or none at all. Investing is often more emotional than logical. That's why people can get into such trouble. I'm surprised doctors don't talk about 'stock-itis.'"

"What's stock-itis?" I asked.

"It's a type of infectious investing. For example, if you caught it, you might feel compelled to invest in a 'hot stock' that everyone else is investing in. It's hard to resist being infected. A classic case of investment infection occurred nearly 400 years ago in Holland."

"Hey Dad," I said, "I thought we already covered the history of cookin' the books."

"No," he said, "we didn't even complete the appetizers.

"Let me tell you what happened in Holland. Amsterdam, the capital city, had become a wealthy city in the 1600s. People started to exhibit their wealth by building large houses. There wasn't much land available so gardens had to be small. The main feature of those gardens was tulips.

"Somehow, everyone of every economic class had to have tulips—and not just any tulips, but the best tulips. Tulip bulb auctions started popping up. Many of the buyers at those auctions didn't want the tulips as flowers to keep and enjoy— they wanted bulbs as a way to make money, big money. Bulbs were being resold for large profits and more people became involved as time went on.

"The Stock Market Crash of 1929 brought on the Great Depression. But the first big market crash was the one in tulips that happened in 1637. Once people woke up and started to wonder why they had traded houses and other valuables for tulip bulbs, the price of bulbs went down fast. Soon, many people had bulbs of little value but no money or houses.

"We laugh at those people who traded their money or houses for a tulip bulb and try to understand how they could have been so gullible. Yet if you look at the New Economy meltdown, it's pretty clear people haven't changed. No matter what century we're in, greed is blinding and infectious."

I hoped listening to Dad would inoculate me and protect me from ever getting stock-itis. The disease sounded pretty serious. It could be fatal to your pocketbook.

#3
Lemons and Lemonade

We sat down at an outdoor cafe and treated ourselves to a couple of lemonades.

The pier was getting more crowded now as people got off work and came down to enjoy the cool sea air and the excitement of the arcade.

The waiter delivered our lemonades. I watched people approach an exhibit, listen to a pitch and either put down their money or walk away. I paid more attention to one pitch in particular because the barker was so much more successful than the rest. How did people decide which game of chance or activity was worthwhile and which ones were a waste of money? This triggered another thought in a similar vein.

"Dad," I asked, "how do you know when you're making a good investment?"

He didn't answer me right away. He moved his lemonade glass around in circles on the table top, retracing the marks left by the condensation of his glass. He was pulling his thoughts together to fit them in a pattern I'd understand and remember. I wasn't surprised by the form of his answer since he had always taught me that people remember stories or vignettes better than they do hard facts.

He started to explain. "The first thing you need to learn in cooking is that the ingredients you put into a dish are the most important factor in getting the right result. You can mask inferior ingredients with sauces or other tricks of the cooking trade, but it always catches up with you. If you don't start out with the purest and best ingredients, you'll be found out in the end. It's the same with companies. Look at their ingredients."

Another technique Dad used was not giving away the answer too easily. He felt that if the listener participated in arriving at the answer, it would be more meaningful and have a greater impact. I knew my next step in this verbal dance.

"What are the investing ingredients to look at?" I asked.

"Well son, that's what we'll be talking about the rest of the evening," he said. "Here's an 'appetizer' to the appetizer. Before you invest in a company, be prepared to explain clearly to a 10-year-old child why it's a good investment. If it's too difficult to explain to a child, there's something wrong with the investment, not the child. Don't try to convince yourself that a lemon is lemonade."

#4
Nothing Stays Fresh Forever—Buy to Sell

Everyday things looked different that night. Off in the horizon we both watched a plane rising up over the ocean after taking off from nearby Los Angeles International Airport. Seeing a plane had a new meaning for me since I'd be on one of those planes tomorrow morning for the biggest adventure of my life.

Dad must've been thinking about the same thing. Dad spoke first. "Almost the first thing that'll happen tomorrow when you get on that plane is that they'll tell you how to get off it. It's funny when you think of it that way. You're strapped in, have no place to go and then they tell you what can go wrong and how to find the emergency exits. It doesn't exactly build confidence in the flying process.

"They're not telling you that something *will* go wrong, just that nothing lasts forever, including airplanes.

"When I go to the wholesale produce markets at the crack of dawn, I'm always looking for the freshest, most pure fruits and vegetables. Every food product has a useable life. After that, they begin to decay. They don't last forever either.

"I don't buy produce to hold onto it. I buy it to sell it—in the dishes I create.

"The same applies to stocks. You buy them knowing that someday you'll sell them. A stock may have its day, its year or its decades. But chances are, over time its luster will fade.

"Fruits and vegetables have a natural life cycle. They grow, they're picked and new ones take their place.

"Companies have life cycles, too. At the beginning, they have a tremendous energy often accompanied by a growth period. Over time, their product may grow too common or stale or oversaturated in the marketplace. Companies may face too much competition or they may grow in unexpected ways or too big to sustain themselves in a healthy way. To be successful in investing, you need to know where a stock is in its life cycle."

I got the gist of it but I still didn't have the guidelines I needed to understand the signs of the corporate life cycle process. I asked, "Dad, how can you tell if a company is in a growth cycle, a dormant cycle or a death cycle?"

He responded. "It's not easy to determine where a company is on its life path. Here's something to help you. When you invest in a company, write down three sentences—why the company was started, what it's doing now and what it will be doing in ten years. You'll be creating in words a description of its path on its life cycle."

"Sounds like," I said, "it's a lot easier to determine a food's life cycle than a company's."

Dad nodded in agreement and added, "All this talk of food reminds me: Be sure to pack up the special meal I cooked for you this morning for the plane ride tomorrow."

I take it back. He did have a little bit of the feminine side, too. Here was the little bit of the mother in him. He was always worried whether I had enough to eat.

Going off to college I wasn't worried about

getting enough to eat there but dorm food was going to be a little tough to swallow after a lifetime of eating at Dad's gourmet kitchen table.

#5
Don't Get Stuck Picking Up the Check

Dad signaled to the waiter to bring our bill.

"A restaurant is like a tidepool," he said. "So much of life is there if you know where to look for it."

He pointed across the restaurant to a large group seated at a huge table. "If they don't all leave at the same time, do you know what will happen?"

I had no idea and I shook my head.

"There are three unwritten rules in the restaurant business with a large group of people. First, the larger the number of diners at a table, the more likely someone is going to end up paying for some or all of someone's else's dinner. Second, he who leaves first never overpays. Third, he who leaves last never has enough money from everyone else to pay the full tip."

"Why's that?" I asked.

Dad responded. "When people leave a table early and give some money for their share, they usually underpay. Whoever is there last has to make good on the bill. Unfortunately, that often means at best there's just enough to cover the food and drinks and only some of the tip."

I had a question. "Is that why some menus say 'A 15% charge will be added for groups of eight or more'?"

He nodded. "That's the only way," he said, "servers of large groups can be assured of receiving a full tip."

Just then one of the four couples got up, left some money on the table and said goodbye. Dad picked up on that and continued, "Likewise if the crowd is leaving a stock, you don't want to be the last one around and have to pick up the tab."

#6
Always Add Up the Check

Our check arrived. Even though we had only ordered two lemonades, Dad studied the check. Old habits are hard to break. He later told me he had this little test. First, he'd ask someone, "Do you look at the itemization on a restaurant bill?" If they said yes, there was a fifty-fifty chance they looked at company annual reports as an investor. If they said no, there was a zero chance. As he put it, "Either you care about details and managing your money or you don't."

I didn't speak up then because I had never reviewed restaurant checks. I guess I was one of the zero chance people.

"Why is it," Dad mused, "if there's an error on your restaurant bill, it's always in favor of the restaurant? And why do the supermarket scanners only make errors that favor the market?"

I didn't have any answers so I shrugged my shoulders.

"And most importantly for your future," he said, "why do errors on corporate financial statements generally overstate income or understate expenses?"

Dad called the waiter over, pointed to the bill and explained that we hadn't ordered any chicken wings. The waiter apologized and took the check back to fix it.

Maybe Dad did know more than me about how things worked in life. I started listening even more carefully. I even later got in the habit of looking over restaurant bills.

Suddenly Dad had a worried look on his face. He spoke to me. "Son, you know my restaurant didn't overcharge. I never permitted that."

I gave him a reassuring smile and answered, "Dad, you're the kind that would leave something off the bill—on purpose."

#7
Is There Cash in the Register?

The waiter came back and placed the corrected bill on the table and walked away. Dad pulled out his wallet to pay it. As he did he motioned for me to look into his wallet. He rifled through several $100 and $20 bills until he found a $5 bill. There must have been almost $500 in there. Then he asked me, "How much cash should I have in my wallet?"

I answered, "It depends what you're using the cash for. Are you making most of your purchases with cash or by check or credit card? I think the answer is 'it depends.'"

He nodded his head and followed up with, "What if I only had $14 in my wallet? Would your answer be the same?"

I shook my head. "No," I said, "obviously you need to walk around with more than $14 in your wallet."

As my dad smiled, he said, "It's the same with corporations. It's not always easy to say how much cash a company needs to have on hand but it's easier to spot when they definitely have too little.

"Now, what if I had $10,000 in cash in my wallet. How would you think I was doing financially?"

I quickly piped up, "You'd be doing great but I wouldn't carry that much cash on me."

He countered, "What if you found out I had just borrowed the $10,000 from a bank?"

I got the point.

"Now," he said, "take the same set of facts and apply them to a company. If cash is going way down, that's a danger sign. How will the company pay its bills? If they don't have enough sales revenue coming in, they'll need to borrow money (and can they?) or possibly issue more stock.

"The craving for cash is one reason companies cook the books. They need to look healthy to qualify for loans and to prevent the loans from being called in for early repayment."

"How's that?" I asked.

Dad continued. "A healthier looking company finds it's easier to get loans and to get a lower interest rate. If companies have enough money, then it's easier for them to borrow money. But if they're really desperate for money, it's hard for them to get it. Also, loans for companies usually have performance clauses that can trigger an early repayment. If a lender sees that a company's revenue or profit is slipping, the loan documents may allow the lender to require repayment right then and there."

And I thought I was facing a lot of pressure entering college and that it would get easier later in life. As Dad talked I could almost feel the pressure to perform bearing down on executives of big companies. But what about the pressure to do the right thing? That was always a hard one for me to resist. Now I knew why: from the time I was a little guy Dad stressed my having a moral compass. He always said that "if you follow the needle pointing to truth and honesty, you'll never get lost."

#8
The Perfect Dessert

Dad paid the check and then we walked to the end of the pier to watch the sunset. No one else was there.

Dad shared that mom and he always enjoyed walking at the beach as the sun went down. They felt so connected to the universe being a part of not only the day turning into night but the ocean meeting the shore. "It was more of a cosmic experience," he explained, "watching a sunset at the beach." That night it felt like the three of us were sharing that sunset.

After the sun got swallowed by the sea, we turned around and walked back from the end of the pier. We had just passed one of those $3 photo booths when Dad retraced his steps. "Let's take some photos together," he said.

This sounded a bit juvenile. I made a face as I said, "The quality won't be very good."

He stepped in the booth, pushed aside the curtain and waved for me to join him. Well, it was his money and he could spend it how he wanted to.

That was the only time I ever saw my Dad make goofy faces in front a camera. It was so unlike him. I couldn't help joining him. It was a lot of fun and we were laughing hard by the time we stepped out. A couple of pre-teen girls waiting to use the booth gave us a look but we didn't care. At that moment I had a glimpse of what he was like before life decided he had the sole responsibility of raising a two-year-son. He was a fun guy.

We sat on a bench and looked and laughed at the photos of the two of us. We each took two to keep. I still carry mine in my wallet to this day.

Not missing a beat, Dad said to me, "A balance sheet is like a still photograph. It shows, on one particular day, what a company has in assets and in liabilities—what it has and what it owes."

"That doesn't sound too informative to me," I blurted out. "What if things change the next day?"

Dad smiled widely. "See. You understand balance sheets. A balance sheet by itself tells you something, but not enough. Balance sheets tell you more when you compare them to each other. If I look at a photograph of you when you were ten, that tells me something. But if I compare it to one of these tonight, I get a fuller picture." Then he pulled out one of the goofy poses. "Over the years you've gotten...ridiculous," he roared.

Still laughing, he talked on. "So just like a single photograph can have valuable, important information, so can a balance sheet. Multiple photographs paint a clearer picture but they don't give you the whole story either. The same is true with balance sheets.

"Let's get back to my wallet and my cash on hand. Cash on hand is an asset on a company's balance sheet. Without enough cash, a company will dry up. Even if the cash situation looks okay, you need to determine *why* it's okay."

I piped up, "Like if the $10,000 in your wallet came from a bank loan."

"Right," he continued. "The first asset you'll see on a balance sheet is cash. You're looking for two things: is there enough on hand now and how much more (or less) is there compared to the cash on the balance sheet three months ago, six months ago and one year ago."

"So in other words, 'show me the money!'" I quipped, mimicking Cuba Gooding Jr.'s line to Tom Cruise in the movie *Jerry Maguire*.

That got a chuckle out of him.

Some of this was making sense but I needed more information to understand balance sheets. "How often is a balance sheet prepared? Do they mail them to you?"

Dad explained. "Companies prepare a balance sheet every three months—that's every quarter—with the fourth one being a recap of the last 12-month period. They're available on the Internet and if you own stock in a company, you'll see their balance sheet as part of an annual report."

I asked, "Does a balance sheet detail the profit or loss?"

"No," he explained, "another financial statement, the income statement, shows that. It details the revenue (what came in), the expenses (what went out) and the amount of profit or loss. Unlike a balance sheet which is a still photo, an income statement covers a longer period of time such as from January 1 through December 31."

He was moving too fast for me. Not only was I foggy on understanding income statements, I still didn't quite get how to track the flow of cash. But I did know how important cash on hand was to me so I guessed that companies didn't want to see an empty wallet either.

I held up my left hand as a stop sign and interrupted him. "Dad," I said, "how can I tell if a company's money came in from its sales or its borrowings?"

Dad responded. "Another financial statement, the statement of cash flow, tells you *where* the money is coming from. Remember, the *amount* of cash may be okay but the source of it may not be ideal. As my mother always said to me, 'Consider the *source*.'"

Dad used to say that a lot to me, too. What I didn't tell him then was that when *he* was the source, I always knew his advice had the best of intentions.

#9
Being Overwhelmed by the Menu

We resumed walking along the arcade. Remembering the father and son playing baseball on the beach, I went over to a stand to try my hand at knocking down some milk bottles with a ball. I was doing pretty well but I needed to blast one more bottle to get a prize. I just couldn't do it.

I was getting frustrated with my pitching and also with some of what Dad was throwing at me.

"Dad, this is getting too complicated. Balance sheet. Income statement. Statement of cash flow. I'm having trouble remembering the names of these financial statements let alone what they are and how to find something wrong with them."

Dad nodded in agreement as he spoke to me. "I'm not expecting you to absorb all of this in one day. I'm trying to give you some tools that you can refer to later on. I'm trying to give you the big picture. I'm not intending to send you out as a forensic accountant to detect fraud."

I interrupted him. "A forensic accountant? What's that?"

Dad responded, "Someone who wears a green eye-shade and uses a pick, a shovel and a microscope."

I didn't get his references so I shrugged my shoulders.

Dad continued. "Some accountants specialize in seeing where the numbers are buried. They're known as forensic accountants. Whenever you hear about the discovery of problems with a financial statement, there's a good chance a forensic accountant found it or uncovered the accounting transactions that show how things got into such a mess.

"I don't expect or want you to be a forensic accountant. What I do want is for you to develop your sense of smell."

"Smell?" I questioned.

Dad nodded. "Develop a sense of what is starting to smell on financial statements, what absolutely stinks and what leaves no unpleasant aroma but makes you question its digestibility. That's what we're doing today. You can't become a forensic accountant in just a few hours."

I felt relieved. Dad wasn't expecting me to become an instant expert on spotting book cookin'. He knew I couldn't even make instant oatmeal without having him first check the expiration date on our fire insurance coverage.

#10
Changing the
Recipe Midstream

We were passing in front of a fortune teller's booth when Dad started talking again.

"Do you remember when I was talking about restated earnings?"

I shook my head. It sounded vaguely familiar.

Dad continued. "I mentioned it in connection with the first way to cook expenses. It's where a company makes a retroactive change to the financial statements. It could be a change to assets, liabilities, in the amount of revenue, a change in the amount of expenses or a change in more than one of these.

"Corporations sometimes act like it's not a big deal to announce 'restated earnings.' But can you imagine how the IRS would react if you or I said, 'Ah, excuse me, we want to restate our earnings for the past five years? Seems we got a little confused about what's income and what's a deductible expense.'"

"Dad," I said, "it seems to me that restating earnings would be like me going back to a professor after an exam and saying I'd like to change some of my answers. But my nose is confused. Is this a real stinker or just a smeller?"

Dad flicked his nose as he responded, "It depends on the circumstances. What's important to remember is that restating earnings should get your nasal attention. Here's another one to get your sniffer going."

My dad was on a roll so I didn't interrupt him.

"Companies make certain assumptions when preparing their financial statements. The assumptions may deal with their method for valuing inventory (there are many different ways), dealing with pension costs or how to account for other items.

"Sometimes companies change their accounting assumptions. A change in assumptions is not necessarily a cause for concern. But recognize that it's a major event on the financial statements. If it's serious business for them, then it's serious business for you if you're investing in the company."

I spoke up here. "How can someone find out what assumptions are being used or changed?"

Dad got a smirk on his face as he answered me. "Do you remember which part of your last history report you hated doing?"

"Yes," I answered, "the footnotes."

"Well," he countered, "history reports aren't the only things in life that have footnotes. So do financial statements like a balance sheet or an income statement or a company's annual report. That's where you find out about a company's assumptions and any changes they're making to them.

"Companies don't make changes lightly in their accounting assumptions. A change usually means someone was wrong about something. If you're using the smell test on financial statements to find suspicious odors, start sniffing here."

#11
Paying for the Next Course

As we continued walking I noticed that my sense of smell was more acute on the pier. Or was it my imagination? To test it, I closed my eyes and tried to distinguish the smells of cooked hamburgers, French fries and fresh fish as well as other less pleasant odors.

Dad gave me a nudge to open my eyes just before I stepped on someone's half-eaten ice cream.

The hamburgers smelled especially good at one stand so Dad and I stopped to sample the wares. We both ordered well-done hamburgers and hoped for the best.

When Dad pulled out his wallet to get some cash, he resumed talking. "Next to cash, the most important asset on a balance sheet may be a company's accounts receivable. As we say in the restaurant biz, 'you want the patron to be able to pay for the next course if he orders it.'"

Dad could see by looking at me I had already forgotten the term "accounts receivable," which we had discussed earlier that day.

"Accounts receivable is the money that's owed to a company that will be paid in the future. That's tomorrow's money. Or next year's money.

"Money is the essential life force of every company. To be successful, a company needs to have enough money on hand today plus a good future flow of cash from its accounts receivable to keep the company afloat. That's why receivables (short for accounts receivable) are so important.

"There are two main tricks that can be played with receivables. First, companies can puff themselves up by counting future revenue now."

"Is there," I asked, "a way to spot this?"

"Sometimes," he answered. "A balance sheet will show two types of accounts receivable: short-term and long-term. Short-term receivables should be paid in no longer than a year. Long-term receivables aren't expected to be paid until more than a year after the date of the balance sheet.

"If long-term receivables are growing real fast, that may be an indicator that the company is wrongfully counting future income today.

"Here's the big picture on this one. Companies estimate how much of the accounts receivable will go bad—that is, become uncollectible. That estimated bad debt expense is a bad debt reserve called an 'allowance for doubtful accounts.' If you see that the company's bad debt reserve is going down but the sales are going up, a bell should be ringing in your head. Usually, the two move together. More sales on credit should mean more bad debts on uncollectible accounts receivable. If a company underestimates its bad debt expense, it's reducing its expenses and inflating income. That's the first trick with receivables."

"What's the second trick?" I asked.

"Smoothing income," he said.

"What's that?" I asked.

Dad told me. "Companies that want to 'save' revenue for another year reduce this year's revenue by pretending some of it is uncollectible. Then later on when it *is* collectible, it's shown as additional income in the later year."

"How is that done?" I inquired.

"Companies make estimates with reserves for the amounts that they expect to write off as an expense," Dad said. "If the reserves turn out to be larger than the estimated costs, the unused reserve is reclassified to increase earnings. If a company plays games with their reserve on accounts receivable, they can manipulate how financial results look in different years. Poorer performing years can be boosted upward and extraordinary years can be toned down."

"Oh yeah," I interjected, "send in the reserves. I remember that now."

Just then we passed a magic act where a ball was being hidden under three cups. People tried to guess where the ball was. They were never right.

"Smoothing income can be done in many ways," Dad explained. "Here's one that doesn't involve accounts receivable. This next one is like a word game. When do expenses mutate to become assets? When they're prepaid expenses.

"Think about it. If an expense is paid in advance, then a company doesn't have to pay the bill when it comes in later. They've already paid for it. When the bill comes in, they just use up part or all of the prepaid expense, the credit balance."

"What's wrong with that?" I asked.

"The problem on financial statements occurs when a company wrongfully transforms future expenses into current expenses and thereby distorts the reporting of current expenses and profit and future expenses and profit."

I interjected, "Pay for the next course after you eat it, not before you sit down at the table?"

Dad nodded in agreement.

#12
Ordering Items
Not on the Menu

We saw some National Guard troops walking on the pier in their camouflage outfits and having a good time.

I thought I'd put my dad to the test and challenge his imagination and improvisational skills. "Dad," I said, "can you work in camouflage in one of your explanations?"

"Piece of cake," he said. He sat for a moment in deep thought. Then he started talking.

"Camouflage is a survival tool in nature. Financial statements have their own forms of camouflage. If you ever see language referring to a 'special purpose entity' or 'SPE' as they're known in the trade, remember that camouflage is a form of concealment. SPEs can be, too."

"What's an SPE?" I asked.

Dad responded. "SPEs are entities that are

formed to interact with a company. Most SPEs have a legitimate and useful purpose. But chances are if there's an SPE, there's also a complicated transaction connected with it. The difficulty is finding out the substance of the transaction and seeing whether it has economic reality or just economic illusion attached to it. SPEs are sometimes 'off-the-record partnerships.'"

This was getting a little complicated for me again so I took advantage of my dad always saying "There's no such thing as a dumb question."

I inquired, "What's an off-the record partnership?"

He replied, "The off-the-record part means the financial substance of what is going on with the partnership isn't fully disclosed on the company's financial statements. Instead, you just see that there is this special purpose entity. The partnership part of this term refers to officers of the company or the company itself being in partnership with outside people or an entity. Why do you think companies use the term 'SPE' instead of 'off-the-record partnership'?"

I remarked, "Even *I* can figure out the strategy

here. Camouflage."

Dad jumped in. "Which one would raise fewer questions? A financial statement that said 'special purpose entity' or one that had an 'off-the record partnership'? A special purpose entity sounds like something good for a company."

He continued. "Remember the round-trip trades we just talked about earlier? That's where two companies, for example, buy and sell gas or power to each other at the same price. The energy doesn't move anywhere but each company treats it like a real sale that boosts revenue.

"Well, some companies supercharge this technique by combining it with 'SPEs' and 'prepays.' Here's how it works.

"The SPE transfers money to the company before anything happens regarding a transfer of energy. It looks like the money is from a prepaid sale of energy, an advance payment. But it isn't. It's a loan to the company. This sale/loan is combined with paper transactions making it look like energy is later transferred (it isn't). So, no energy moves anywhere and a loan is disguised as a sale."

I spoke up. "Do you actually expect me to understand this? This is way too complicated."

Dad nodded reassuringly to me. "You've hit upon the essence of some SPEs. Camouflage through complication. If transactions are designed to be so complex that officers and directors can't understand them, they have a better chance of sneaking through the corporate approval process.

"Often times when you see an SPE, the officers and directors who aren't involved in setting up the SPE really don't understand what's going on either. It's like approving a menu but not knowing all the dishes that will be served off it.

"Let me give it one more try to explain this," he replied. "Putting all the pieces together, the company makes it look like it has increased revenue (it hasn't) by making a sale (it didn't) to a related company it helped set up to increase its assets (it hasn't) by treating a loan like it was prepaid income (it isn't). To add insult to injury, the company doesn't treat it like income on its corporate tax returns. There it shows it as a debt. As they say in the energy trade, 'now they're cooking with gas.'"

My head was spinning. I had trouble understanding how I could interpret games being played with items that were *on* the company books and records. How could anyone unravel what was happening with *off*-the-books partnerships and entities?

Taking American literature this fall didn't sound so tough now. Look at all these tips I was being given on how to interpret fiction.

#13
Ice Cream Redux

We saw another ice cream vendor. That reminded me of our earlier discussion of ice cream and inventory.

"Dad, how can inventory be manipulated?" I asked.

"Every item on a balance sheet can be manipulated," he said. "Take inventory. What are the danger signs? First, compare the growth rate of sales and inventory. If inventory is growing faster, the company may be overstocking inventory or counting unsalable inventory that should've been written off as an expense."

I interrupted and asked, "Do you mean spoiling, like rotten fruit?"

Dad nodded and said, "Yes. That's one way. Another way is for inventory becoming obsolete. A clothing manufacturer or department store chain may have too much of last year's fashion clothing. That inventory may need to be marked down or written off entirely.

Second, just as with receivables, companies set up reserves for inventory going bad. Just as games can be played with reserves for accounts receivable, they can be with inventory."

For the rest of my life every time I saw melted ice cream I said to myself, "More inventory going bad."

#14
Acquisition Indigestion
Buying Ingredients Isn't the Same as Selling Dinners

We passed by a nice Italian restaurant with outdoor tables. A very well-dressed man walked over to a table, smiled and spoke a few words to the diners. He must have gotten a good response because he smiled again before he walked off to another table to repeat the process.

Dad pointed over there and said, "I'll bet you that's the owner of the restaurant. He's really concerned whether his customers are being treated well.

"Some owners avoid their customers. That's a mistake. If I had spent all my time as a restaurant owner buying supplies and ingredients and not spending time cooking, checking up on and taking care of my customers, my restaurant would have been in a heap of trouble.

"It's like that in the corporate world, too. Watch out for companies whose main business seems to be buying and selling other companies and not operating them.

"Sometimes these companies bury their financial disasters by combining so many different types of companies into one main set of financial statements, it's difficult to figure out what went right and what went wrong and on whose watch it happened.

"So, take a financial physical of a company before you invest in it. See where the company started. What field of business was it in? Has it stayed there? If it has expanded into other industries, do the various companies it owns work together to build something better or just something bigger? Do the executives have a reputation for cutting and burning or for sticking around for the longer term? Acquisitions can be a way to hide deficiencies. Watch out!"

All this from Dad just watching that man walk from one table to the next. Pretty sharp guy, my dad.

#15
Overcharging
on the Menu

We heard an accordion player at the restaurant
and Dad started singing along with the music,
"When the expense hits your eye like a big pizza
pie, that's amori...tization."

I didn't recognize the tune or that word,
"amortization."

Dad explained that the former was a big hit in
the 1960s and the latter can cause big financial
hits.

"Amortization is a hard concept to understand
probably because the word itself isn't commonly
used in everyday talk," he said.

"Intangible assets have a limited life. What's an
intangible asset you want to ask? Examples of
these assets are patents and copyrights. They are
granted for a limited period of time. After that,
it's fair game for anyone using the patented or
copyrighted items.

"Because the protection for those assets runs out over time, it's considered correct to recognize the annual reduction of value of these assets through an expense called amortization. No problem with amortizing those assets if the correct number of years for their useful life is selected. Sometimes you'll see the words 'depreciating' and 'amortizing' used interchangeably. They both involve writing down the value of assets on the company books."

"So," I asked, "where can there be a big problem amortizing or writing down the value of assets?"

"Goodwill," he answered.

"Goodwill?" I asked. "What's that?"

My dad explained. "If one company buys another and they can't justify allocating all of the costs to each of the purchased assets, then what's left over is called goodwill.

"Goodwill is sort of a catch-all asset when you run out of containers in acquiring another company.

"Until recently, companies amortized goodwill,

145

deducting a set amount each year. The new accounting rule says 'keep it on the financial statements as is until its value goes down.' If a company later determines or discovers what they bought isn't as valuable as they thought, they need to reduce the asset called goodwill and take an expense."

I started scratching my head. "Dad," I asked, "how do companies know exactly how much to allocate to each asset when they acquire a company and how much to say is leftover as goodwill?"

"They don't exactly," he said. "That gives wiggle room to later play with goodwill expense to affect profits in the current reporting period and down the road. One rainy-day accounting technique is to write down goodwill in the current period to make future periods look better.

"Because goodwill can often be a huge item and it can be highly discretionary to determine when assets have lost their value and how much value they've lost, put this one on your list to watch."

I didn't have the heart to tell him that I wasn't making a list. I was listening, not listing.

#16
Where's the Beef?

We passed by another restaurant that had its menu on display out front. I had never in my life seen such a long or complicated menu. It made me think of some of the financial documents Dad had been talking about. They were probably all too complicated for me to understand.

"Dad," I asked, "where do you go looking for accounting tricks and fraud?"

"If you're huntin' for financial clues," he explained, "concentrate your search on these documents:

1. Annual report to shareholders
2. Annual report to the SEC (Form 10-K)
3. Quarterly reports to the SEC (Form 10-Q)
4. SEC form to report certain sales of stocks (Form 144)
5. SEC form to report significant events or corporate changes of importance to investors (Form 8-K)
6. SEC forms on the stock ownership, purchases and sales for every director, officer and 10%

147

(or larger) owner (Forms 3, 4 and 5)
7. The auditor's report

"And these are just the beginning. Another good one is the proxy statement mailed to shareholders each year with the announcement of the annual shareholder's meeting."

"Dad," I asked, "where can anyone find this stuff?"

"The Internet makes it easy. Go to www.sec.gov to see SEC filings. What I always find of particular interest is whether company officials are selling. I don't want to be the last person aboard a sinking ship.

"Each annual report to shareholders, which is mailed by a company, includes not only vital financial information but also a narrative telling where the company has been, how things are going and where it's going.

"An auditor's report also often makes interesting reading."

Well, he read recipes for a living. Maybe an auditor's report really helped spice up his life.

Dad continued. "The report should note any special circumstances that make the auditor uneasy about the company's operations or prospects. Over time, auditors will probably voice any concerns or even suspicions.

"Some of the most interesting, tasty and important reading in financial information is in the footnotes.

"That's where the juicy stuff is usually located. You may see information about company sales or acquisitions of other companies that cast a whole new light on what's going on with the company.

"Want to find out about other related entities that are used as financial landfills to bury expenses? Look at the footnotes."

I was remembering how this whole afternoon and evening's discussion got started. "Dad," I inquired, "where can someone find out about the stock options a company has issued?"

"Unless a company has jumped on the bandwagon to fuller disclosure right in the body of the financial statements, look at the footnotes to see how a corporation would really be doing if they counted stock options as expenses. And, even if they count options as expenses, the footnotes will tell you what method they're using to value the options."

"You mean," I said, "there's more than one way to value options?"

"Of course," he responded, "remember that much of accounting is not black or white."

"Here's my final word on footnotes. It's not the point size of the type that indicates the importance of information. It's the dollar size in its details that counts.

"Son, there's lots more to know about financial statements and finding out what's right or not right on them. There are all sorts of numbers and ratios to look at: EPS, EBITDA, P/E ratio, the quick ratio, this ratio, that ratio. These are all valuable tools but don't worry about them tonight."

Don't worry, Dad. Heck, if I couldn't find a hamburger on that menu outside that restaurant, I wasn't counting on being a ratio expert that night.

#17
Make Sure the Flavor Isn't Too Diluted

We stood outside the restaurant watching a waiter come up to a table and start to mix the dressing for a salad right on the spot.

Dad nodded in approval. "Mixing a great salad dressing is really an art form. You need the proper balance of ingredients. If you water down the mixture, the original flavor becomes lost and unappealing. In a similar way, stocks can be diluted, watered down, by too many stock options.

"What happens to a stock option if the stock's value is more than the option's cost?" he asked me.

I shrugged my shoulders. "Well," he continued, "chances are the option will turn into shares of stock. That means the company will issue more shares of stock."

"That's good," I said.

"Why do you think that?" he asked.

"Because," I answered, "more people are interested in the stock of a company and owning some stock in it."

Since I wasn't getting his point Dad looked around for another way of explaining it. He pointed to a table in the corner.

"See that table where the wine is being served?" he said. I nodded yes.

"Pretend each of those people at the table is a stockholder and pretend that the bottle of wine is the profits. Okay so far?"

I nodded again.

"If more people come to the table and ask to have some wine, what happens to the first people at the table?" he asked.

"Obviously, they have less to drink," I responded. Then I got it and I explained it to my dad.

"The first people at the table are the existing shareholders. The people who join them are the ones who used their options to join the shareholder party. Having new, additional shareholders means the same bottle of wine has to be split among more glasses. The same amount of wine, profits, has to be divided up among more shareholders. The options dilute the profits for the original shareholders. I got it."

Dad echoed me, "You got it! Before you plunk down your investment dollars, check out the potential dilution size. Oh, yeah, the footnotes to the financial statements will be the best place to spot how many shares may be issued to these new fellow shareholders."

#18
Don't Forget to Include the Taxes

Something Dad had said earlier was still gnawing at me. "Dad, when you were talking about SPEs you mentioned income taxes. Are games played with taxes, too?"

Dad nodded with his lips clenched. "One way corporations can improve their bottom line is by reducing their income tax burden.

"As with accounting rules, everything in taxes is not clear-cut. The old smell test works here, too."

"How?" I asked.

Dad responded. "It's interesting. The same aspects that often provide a tell-tale odor to corporate accounting practices also apply to tax gimmicks: 1) numerous paper transactions with no real-life significance, 2) the creation of many entities to camouflage what's really happening and 3) being too good to be true (generating deductions that dwarf the original investment in the case of taxes and inflated revenue or profits or deflated expenses in the case of accounting books and records). A real stinker of a transaction will have all three."

I was getting very disillusioned about corporate accounting at this point and told my dad so.

He explained. "Even though the GAAP rules are thousands of pages, the rules don't cover everything. More importantly, the rules give accountants flexibility. Accounting is part art and part science. It's not just one plus one equals two. Accountants need to use their discretion and judgment in setting up accounting systems and there's no one type of accounting system that will work right for every corporation."

"Why not?" I asked.

"Here's why," he said. "If you become a video game consultant, you'll be able to account for your business by the checks you write and the checks you deposit.

"You would have mostly short-term or up-to-one-year contracts to provide services. It'd be pretty easy to match up your income and expenses. You could use your cash-in, cash-out method for them okay.

"However, it's a different story for the video game manufacturer.

"The product cycle here starts with maybe years of research and development to develop a salable product. Then once orders are placed, it takes time to set up the manufacturing plants and produce the games. The games would be produced at different times—some this year, some next year and so on for a period of years. Then stores or a distributor for the video game company might have a lengthy period of time to pay for the games they're selling.

"When should the expenses of the video game manufacturer be counted? Mainly up front during the early years? When should revenue be counted? When a contract is signed to sell games to a chain, when the games are actually delivered or when they're finally paid for?

"Should your one-man consulting company and the video game manufacturer report revenue and expenses the same way or will that distort the results?

"This is where companies need the wisdom and judgment of their accountants in coming up with an accounting system that properly matches revenue and expenses.

"Of course, the devil is in the details," he said, "since there is often wiggle room to put a different cast on financial results. That's why we need our traditional accountants—the honest ones."

#19
The Secret
Ingredients

At this point, I had to ask a question that had been running through my mind all day. "How common is it for companies to just plain lie?"

"Not as common as some people think and more common than others could imagine," he told me.

"Although it's rare, corporate officials, for example, sometimes claim phony sales to boost revenue."

I spoke up again. "Why? Don't they have a conscience?"

"It could be greed," Dad said. "It could be keeping up with the Joneses. If corporate officers with other companies are flashing tremendous wealth and having it result in getting publicity for themselves and their companies, that can be a temptation to emulate. The problem can come if a company doesn't generate enough legitimate wealth to get this publicity. Maybe it can be rationalized by these company officials that cookin' the books to generate this similar exposure and interest is all for the company good.

"It's just a by-product that the chefs in charge get super wealthy in making this recipe work.

"Little lies can lead to bigger lies and those lies can make it easier to make the Big Lie in corporate accounting—phony sales.

"How do you spot a corporate liar? Use what we've talked about today as a starting point and don't put on blinders when you invest. See things as they are. Not as you want them to be."

#20
The Last Item
on the Menu

We passed a cookie store.

Dad piped up, "A good fudge recipe calls for a healthy portion of sugar. If a chef tries to sweeten the fudge too much though, the result is a disaster. Financial reporting can suffer from excess, too. If a company is engaged in 'aggressive financial reporting,' you can bet dollars to doughnuts that there's some hanky panky going on."

Then he gave me his final piece of advice that day. Words to live by. "Fudge is good—fudging isn't."

Epilogue

Epilogue
(Sometime in the Future)

Here I am holding hands with my wife and our five-year-old son and walking along that same Southern California beach. Holding my son's other hand is my dad.

Many years have passed since that college-eve walk with him. Last night we were talking about the changes that put most of the book cookers out of business:

• Mutual funds and state retirement plans that hold a fortune in stocks now require companies to have more transparent and accurate accounting procedures or face the risk of a mass pullout of those investment funds—or as Dad puts it, "Money talks, especially if it walks."

• There are tougher laws and stronger enforcement by the SEC as well as state attorneys general—Dad's take on this is that "Most company officers would see the risk of 20 years in prison for a one-year gain in profits as a bad trade."

• Insurance companies refuse to issue errors and omissions policies for corporate directors unless the highest accounting standards are followed, strong internal controls are imposed and independent boards of directors are active in being diligent—according to Dad, "There's nothing like personal liability to make someone sit up and pay attention."

• And maybe, most importantly, accountants now walk away from clients that don't follow the rules and the public knows why they've dropped a client—Dad's final cookism is: "How nice it is to have accountants doing business the old-fashioned way. If you are willing to say 'no' to someone and accept the consequences, it empowers you."

So things are getting better. But someday I'll have the same walk and talk with my son to make him more savvy about corporate accounting and life in general. Caveat emptor may be old advice but it's timeless.

I've put Dad's advice to good use as I've expanded the video game manufacturing company I started. The only cookin' we do at my company is when we come up with great ideas and figure out how to implement them.

And Dad? Shortly after our walk years ago, he stopped being a corporate chef. He opened his own restaurant again, this time on the pier. He doesn't cook as much anymore. If you ever come to his restaurant, walk up to him to say hello or just sit and wait. He'll find you. Every night he goes from table to table making sure everything is just right for the customers.

I had a present for Dad at the end of our walk that day. I gave him a copy of this book with this dedication written in it:

To Dad,

The greatest chef in the world. I want to share the advice you gave me to make sure no one gets their goose cooked in the stock market.

Love,

The Head Chef's Son

About the Author

Don Silver is a personal finance writer, editor, columnist, author and Internet content provider. He is the author of eight books including *Baby Boomer Retirement*, *The Generation X Money Book*, *The Generation Y Money Book* and *A Parent's Guide to Wills and Trusts*.

Silver passed the written CPA examination and practiced law for over two decades before devoting all of his time to writing.

As a regular ongoing columnist on *Quicken.com*'s Retirement Channel and Microsoft's *Money-Insider*, Silver wrote about important personal finance and retirement topics with a wry sense of humor. He has been featured on the *NBC Network News*, *CNNfn*, *Associated Press*, *USA Weekend*, *Reuters* and *America Online*.

Silver has a broad range of writing skills. He is also a technical writer and editor and writes online and hardcopy computer manuals.

Although Silver is a dad, he is *not* the dad in this book. Cooking scrambled eggs is the limit of his talent in the kitchen. His wife can testify to that.

Index

Index

172